THE SEVEN SAYINGS OF THE SAVIOR ON THE CROSS

ARTHUR PINK

Paperback: 978-939492408-6

Sanage Publishing House LLP
Mumbai, India

sanagepublishing@gmail.com

Arthur Walkington Pink (1886 – 1952) was an English Bible teacher who sparked a renewed interest in the exposition of Calvinism or Reformed Theology. Little known in his own lifetime, Pink became "one of the most influential evangelical authors in the second half of the twentieth century."

His writing sparked a revival of expository preaching and focused readers' hearts on biblical living.

CONTENTS

INTRODUCTION

The death of the Lord Jesus Christ is a subject of never-failing interest to all who study prayerfully the Scripture of Truth. This is so not only because the believer's all, both for time and eternity, depends upon it, but also because of its transcendent uniqueness. Four words appear to sum up the salient features of this mystery of mysteries: the death of Christ was natural, unnatural, preternatural, and supernatural. A few comments seem called for by way of definition and amplification.

First, the death of Christ was natural. By this we mean that it was a real death. It is because we are so familiar with the fact of it that the above statement appears simple and commonplace, yet what we hear touch upon is to the spiritual mind one of the main elements of wonderment. The One who was "taken, and by wicked hands" crucified and slain was none less than Immanuel (Act 2:23). The One who died on Calvary's Cross was none other than Jehovah's "fellow" (Zechariah 13:7). The blood that was shed on the accursed tree was divine "The church of God which he purchased with his own blood" (Act 20:28). As says the apostle, "God was in Christ, reconciling the world unto himself" (2 Corinthians 5:19).

But how could Jehovah's "fellow" suffer? How could the eternal One die? Ah, He who in the beginning was the Word, who was with God, and who was God, "became flesh." He who was in the form of God took upon Him the form of a servant and was made in the likeness of men; "and being found in fashion as a man, he humbled himself, and became obedient unto death, even the death of the cross" (Phi 2:8). Thus, having become incarnate, the Lord of glory was capable of suffering death, and so it was that He "tasted" death itself. In His words, "Father, into your hands I commend my spirit," we see how natural His death was. The reality of it became still more apparent when He was laid in the tomb, where He remained for three days.

Second, the death of Christ was un-natural. By this we mean that it was abnormal. Above we have said that in becoming incarnate, the Son of God became capable of suffering death. Yet it must not be inferred from this that death therefore had a claim upon Him; far from this being the case, the very reverse was the truth. Death is the wages of sin, and He had none. Before His birth it was said to Mary, "that holy thing which shall be born of you shall be called the Son of God" (Luke 1:35). Not only did the Lord Jesus enter this world without contracting the defilement attaching to fallen human nature, but He "did no sin" (1 Peter 2:22), had "no sin" (1 John 3:5), "knew no sin" (2 Corinthians 5:21). In His person and in His conduct, He was the Holy One of God "without blemish and without spot" (1 Peter 1:19). As such, death had no claim upon Him. Even Pilate had to acknowledge that he could find in Him "no fault." Hence, we say, for the Holy One of God to die was un-natural.

Third, the death of Christ was preternatural. By this we mean that it was marked out and determined for Him beforehand. He was the Lamb slain from the foundation of the world (Rev 13:8). Before Adam was created, the Fall was anticipated. Before sin entered the world, salvation from it had been planned by God. In the eternal counsels of Deity, it was fore-ordained that there should be a Savior for sinners, a Savior Who should suffer, the Just for the unjust, a Savior Who should die in order that we might live. And "because there was none other good enough to pay the price for sin," the only Begotten of the Father offered Himself as the Ransom.

The preternatural character of the death of Christ has been well termed the "undergirding of the Cross." It was in view of that approaching death that God "justly passed over the sins done a foretime" (Rom 3:25 R.V.) Had not Christ been, in the reckoning of God, the Lamb slain from the foundation of the world, every sinning person in the Old Testament times would have gone down to the Pit the moment he sinned!

Fourth, the death of Christ was supernatural. By this we mean that it was different from every other death. In all things He has the pre-eminence. His birth was different from all other births. His life was different from all other lives. And His death was different from all other deaths. This was clearly intimated in His own utterance upon the subject "Therefore does my Father love me, because I lay down my life, that I might take it again. No man takes it from me, but I lay it down of myself. I have power...to take it again" (John 10:17-18). A careful study of the Gospel narratives which describe His death furnish a sevenfold proof and verification of His assertion.

(1) That our Lord "laid down his life," that He was not powerless in the hands of His enemies, comes out clearly in John 18, where we have the record of His arrest. A band of officers from the chief priests and Pharisees, headed by Judas, sought Him in Gethsemane. Coming forward to meet them, the Lord Jesus asks, "Whom seek you?" The reply was, "Jesus of Nazareth," and then our Lord uttered the ineffable title of deity, that by which Jehovah had revealed Himself of old to Moses at the burning bush "I AM." The effect was startling. We are told "they went backward and fell to the ground." These officers were awestruck. They were in the presence of incarnate Deity and were overpowered by a brief consciousness of divine majesty. How plain it is then that had He so pleased, our blessed Savior could have walked quietly away, leaving those who had come to arrest Him prostrate on the ground! Instead, He delivers Himself up into their hands and is led (not driven) as a lamb to the slaughter.

(2) Let us now turn to Matthew 27:46, the most solemn verse in all the Bible "And about the ninth hour Jesus cried with a loud voice,

saying, Eli, Eli, lama, sabachthani? that is to say, My God, my God, why have you forsaken me?" The words which we would ask the reader to observe carefully are here placed in italics. Why is it that the Holy Spirit tells us that the Savior uttered that terrible cry "with a loud voice"? Most certainly there is a reason for it. This becomes even more apparent when we note that He has repeated them four verses lower down in the same chapter "Jesus, when he had cried again with a loud voice, yielded up the spirit" (Mat 27:50). What then do these words indicate? Do they not corroborate what has been said in the above paragraphs? Do they not tell us that the Savior was not exhausted by what He had passed through? Do they not intimate that His strength had not failed Him? that He was still master of Himself, that instead of being conquered by death, He was but yielding Himself to it? Do they not show us that God had "laid help upon one that was mighty" (Psalm 89:19)!

(3) We call attention next to His fourth utterance on the Cross "I thirst." This word, in the light of its setting, furnishes a wonderful evidence of our Lord's complete self-possession. The whole verse reads as follows: "After this, Jesus knowing that all things were now accomplished, that the scripture might be fulfilled, said, I thirst" (John 19:28). Of old it had been predicted that they should give the Savior to drink vinegar mingled with gall. And in order that this prophecy might be fulfilled, He cried, "I thirst." How this evidences the fact that He was in full possession of His mental faculties, that His mind was unclouded, that His terrible sufferings had neither deranged nor disturbed it. As He hung on the Cross, at the close of the six hours, His mind reviewed the entire scope of the prophetic word and checked off one by one those predictions which had reference to His passion. Excepting the prophecies which were to be fulfilled after His death, but one remained un-fulfilled, namely, "They gave me also gall for my meat; and in my thirst they gave me vinegar to drink" (Psalm 69:21), and this was not overlooked by the blessed Sufferer. "Jesus knowing that all things were now accomplished, that the scripture (not "scriptures," the reference being to Psalm 69:21) might be

fulfilled, says, I thirst." Again, we say, what proof is here furnished that He "laid down his life" of Himself (1 John 3:16)!

(4) The next verification the Holy Spirit has supplied of our Lord's words in John 10:18 is found in John 19:30 "When Jesus had received the vinegar, he said, It is finished; and he bowed his head, and gave up the spirit." What are we intended to learn from these words? What is here signified by this act of the Savior? Surely the answer is not far to seek. The implication is clear. Previous to this our Lord's head had been held erect. It was no impotent sufferer that hung there in a swoon. Had that been the case His head had lolled helplessly on His chest, and it would have been impossible for Him to "bow" it. And mark attentively the verb used here: it is not His head "fell," but He consciously, calmly, reverently bowed His head. How sublime was His carriage even on the tree! What superb composure did He evidence? Was it not His majestic bearing on the Cross that, among other things, caused the centurion to cry "Truly this was the son of God" (Mat 27:54)!

(5) Look now at His last act of all: "And when Jesus had cried with a loud voice, he said, Father, into your hands I commend my spirit: and having said this, he gave up the spirit" (Luke 23:46). None else ever did this or died thus. How accurately these words agree with His own statement, so often quoted by us, "I lay down my life, that I might take it again. No man takes it from me, but I lay it down of myself "(John 10:17-18). The uniqueness of our Lord's action may be seen by comparing His words on the Cross with those of dying Stephen. As the first Christian martyr came to the brink of the river, he cried, "Lord Jesus, receive my spirit" (Act 7:59). But in contrast with this, Christ said, "Father into your hands I commend my spirit." Stephen's spirit was being taken from him. Not so with the Savior. None could take from Him His life. He "gave up" His spirit.

(6) The action of the soldiers in regard to the legs of those on the three crosses gives further evidence of the uniqueness of Christ's death. We read, "The Jews therefore, because it was the preparation,

that the bodies should not remain upon the Cross on the Sabbath day, (for that Sabbath day was a high day), besought Pilate that their legs might be broken, and that they might be taken away. Then came the soldiers, and break the legs of the first, and of the other which was crucified with him. But when they came to Jesus, and saw that he was dead already, they brake not his legs" (John 19:31-33).

The Lord Jesus and the two thieves had been crucified together. They had been on their respective crosses the same length of time. And now at the close of the day the two thieves were still alive, for as it is well known that death by crucifixion, though exceedingly painful, was usually a slow death. No vital member of the body was directly affected, and often the sufferer lingered on for two or three days before being completely overcome by exhaustion. It was not natural, therefore, that Christ should be dead after but six hours on the Cross. The Jews recognized this and requested Pilate that the legs of all three be broken and death thus be hastened. In the fact, then, that the Savior was "dead already" when the soldiers came to Him, though the two thieves yet lived, we have additional proof that He had voluntarily "laid down his life" of Himself, that it was not "taken from him."

(7) For the final demonstration of the super-natural character of Christ's death we turn to note the wonderful phenomena that accompanied it, "And behold, the veil of the temple was rent in twain from the top to the bottom; and the earth did quake, and the rocks rent; and the graves were opened" (Mat 27:51-52). That was no ordinary death that had been witnessed on the summit of Golgotha's rugged heights, and it was followed by no ordinary attendants. First, the veil of the temple was rent in twain from top to bottom, to show that a Hand from Heaven had torn asunder that curtain which shut out the temple-worshiper from the earthly throne of God thus signifying that the way into the Holiest was now made plain and that access to God Himself had been opened up through the broken body of His Son. Next, the earth did quake. Not, I believe, that there was

an earthquake, nor even a "great earthquake," but the earth itself, the entire earth was shaken to its very foundation, and rocked on its axis, as though to show it was horrified at the most awful deed that had ever been perpetrated on its surface. "And the rocks rent" the very strength of nature gave way before the greater power of that death. Finally, we are told, "the graves were opened," showing that the power of Satan, which is death, was there shivered and shattered all the outward attestations of the value of that atoning death.

Putting these together: the manifest yielding up of Himself into the hands of those who arrested Him; the crying with a "loud voice," denoting His retained vigour; the fact that He was in full and unimpaired possession of His mentality, evidenced by the "knowing that all things were now accomplished"; the "bowing" of the erect head; the deliberate "committing" of His spirit into the hands of the Father; the fact that He was "dead already" when the soldiers came to brake His legs all furnished proof that His life was not taken from Him, but that He laid it down of Himself. This, together with the tearing of the temple veil, the quaking of the earth, the rending of the rocks, and the opening of the graves, all bore unmistakable witness to the supernatural character of His death; in view of which we may well say with the wondering centurion, "Truly this was the son of God" (Mat 27:54).

The death of Christ, then, was unique, miraculous, supernatural. In the chapters which follow we shall hearken to the words which fell from His lips while He hung upon the Crosswords which make known to us some of the attendant circumstances of the great tragedy; words which reveal the excellencies of the One who suffered there; words in which is wrapped up the Gospel of our salvation; and words which inform us of the purpose, the meaning, the sufferings, and the sufficiency of the death divine.

1. The Word Of Forgiveness

"Then said Jesus, Father, forgive them; for they know not what they do." Luke 23:34

Man had done his worst. The One by Whom the world was made had come into it, but the world knew Him not. The Lord of Glory had tabernacled among men, but He was not wanted. The eyes which sin had blinded saw in Him no beauty that He should be desired. At His birth there was no room in the inn, which foreshadowed the treatment He was to receive at the hands of men. Shortly after His birth Herod sought to slay Him, and this intimated the hostility His person evoked and forecast the Cross as the climax of man's enmity. Again, and again His enemies attempted His destruction. And now their vile desires have granted them. The Son of God had yielded Himself up into their hands. A mock trial had been gone through, and though His judges found no fault in Him, nevertheless, they had yielded to the insistent clamouring of those who hated Him as they cried again and again, "Crucify him."

The fell deed had been done. No ordinary death would suffice for His implacable foes. A death of intense suffering and shame was decided upon. A cross had been secured; the Savior had been nailed to it. And there He hangs, silent. But presently His pallid lips are seen to move

Is He crying for pity? No. What then? Is He pronouncing malediction upon His crucifiers? No. He is praying, praying for His enemies "Then said Jesus, Father, forgive them: for they know not what they do" (Luke 23:34).

The first of the seven cross-sayings of our Lord presents Him in the attitude of prayer. How significant! How instructive! His public ministry had opened with prayer (Luke 3:21), and here we see it closing in prayer. Surely, He has left us an example! No longer might those hands minister to the sick, for they are nailed to the Cross; no longer may those feet carry Him on errands of mercy, for they are fastened to the cruel tree; no longer may He engage in instructing the apostles, for they have forsaken Him and fled how then does He occupy Himself? In the ministry of prayer! What a lesson for us.

Perhaps these lines may be read by some who by reason of age and sickness are no longer able to work actively in the Lord's vineyard. Possibly in days gone by, you were a teacher, you were a preacher, a Sunday-school teacher, a tract distributor but now you are bed-ridden. Yes, but you are still here on earth! Who knows but what God is leaving you here for a few more days to engage in the ministry of prayer and perhaps accomplish more by this than all your past active service? If you are tempted to disparage such a ministry, remember your Savior. He prayed, prayed for others, prayed for sinners, even in His last hours.

In praying for His enemies, not only did Christ set before us a perfect example of how we should treat those who wrong and hate us, but He also taught us never to regard any as beyond the reach of prayer. If Christ prayed for His murderers, then surely, we have encouragement to pray now for the very chief of sinners! Christian reader, never lose hope. Does it seem a waste of time for you to continue praying for that man, that woman, that wayward child of yours? Does their case seem to become more hopeless every day? Does it look as though they had gotten beyond the reach of divine mercy? Perhaps that one you have prayed for so long has been ensnared by one of the Satanic cults of the day, or he may now be an avowed and blatant infidel, in a word, an open enemy of Christ. Remember then the Cross. Christ prayed for His enemies. Learn then not to look on any as beyond the reach of prayer.

One more thought concerning this prayer of Christ. We are shown here the efficacy of prayer. This Cross-intercession of Christ for His enemies met with a marked and definite answer. The answer is seen in the conversion of three thousand souls on the day of Pentecost. I base this conclusion on Acts 3:17, where the apostle Peter says, "And now, brethren, I know that through ignorance you did it, as did also your rulers." It is to be noted that Peter uses the word "ignorance," which corresponds with our Lord's "they know not what they do." Here then is the divine explanation of the three thousand converted under a single sermon. It was not Peter's eloquence which was the cause, but the Savior's prayer.

And Christian reader, the same is true of us. Christ prayed for you and me long before we believed in Him. Turn to John 17:20 for proof: "Neither pray I for these (the apostles) alone, but for them also which shall believe on me through their word" (John 17:20). Once more let us profit from the perfect Exemplar. Let us to make intercession for the enemies of God, and if we pray in faith we also shall pray effectively unto the salvation of lost sinners.

To come now directly to our text: "Then said Jesus, Father, forgive them for they know not what they do."

1. Here we see the fulfilment of the prophetic word. How much God made known beforehand of what should transpire on the day of days! What a complete picture did the Holy Spirit furnish of our Lord's Passion with all the attendant circumstances! Among other things it had been foretold that the Savior should "make intercession for the transgressors" (Isa 53:12). This did not have reference to the present ministry of Christ at God's right hand. It is true that "He is able also to save them to the uttermost that come unto God by him,

seeing he ever lives to make intercession for them" (Heb 7:25), but this speaks of what He is doing now for those who have believed on Him, whereas Isaiah 53:12 had reference to His gracious act at the time of His crucifixion. Observe what His intercession for the transgressors is there linked with "And he was numbered with the transgressors; and he bare the sin of many and made intercession for the transgressors."

That Christ should make intercession for His enemies was one of the items of the wonderful prophecy found in Isaiah 53. This chapter tells us at least ten things about the humiliation and suffering of the Redeemer. It declared that He should be despised and rejected of men; that He should be a Man of sorrows and acquainted with grief; that He should be wounded, bruised and chastised; that He should be led, unresistingly, to slaughter; that He should be dumb before His shearers; that He should not only suffer at the hands of man but also be bruised by the Lord; that He should pour out His soul unto death; that He should be buried in a rich man's tomb; and then it was added, that He would be numbered with transgressors. Here then was the prophecy "and made intercession for the transgressors"; there was the fulfilment of it "Father, forgive them, for they know not what they do." He thought of His murderers; He pleaded for His crucifiers; He made intercession for their forgiveness.

"Then said Jesus, Father, forgive them, for they know not what they do."

2. Here we see Christ identified with His people. "Father, forgive them." On no previous occasion did Christ make such a request of the Father. Never before had He invoked the Father's forgiveness of others. Hitherto He Himself forgave. To the man sick of palsy, He had said, "Son, be of good cheer; your sins be forgiven you" (Mat 9:2). To the woman who washed His feet with her tears in the house of Simon, He said, "Your sins are forgiven" (Luke 7:48). Why then should He now ask the Father to forgive, instead of directly pronouncing forgiveness Himself?

Forgiveness of sins is a divine prerogative. The Jewish scribes were right when they reasoned "Who can forgive sins but God only" (Mar 2:7). But you say, Christ was God. Truly, but man also the Godman. He was the Son of God that had become the Son of Man, with the express purpose of offering Himself as a sacrifice for sins. And when the Lord Jesus cried "Father forgive them," He was on the Cross, and there He might not exercise His divine prerogatives. Mark carefully His own words, and then behold the marvellous accuracy of Scripture. He had said, "The Son of Man has power on earth to forgive sins" (Mat 9:6). But He was no longer on earth! He had been "lifted up from the earth" (John 12:32)! Moreover, on the Cross He was acting as our substitute: the Just was about to die for the unjust. Hence it was that, hanging there as our representative, He was no longer in the place of authority where He might exercise His own divine prerogatives. Therefore, He takes the position of a suppliant before the Father. Thus, we say that when the blessed Lord Jesus cried, "Father, forgive them," we see Him absolutely identified with His people. No longer was He in the position "on earth" where He had the "power" or "right" to forgive sins; instead, He intercedes for sinners as we must.

"Then said Jesus, Father, forgive them, for they know not what they do."

3. Here we see the divine estimate of sin and its consequent guilt. Under the Levitical economy God required that atonement should be made for sins of ignorance. "If a soul commit a trespass, and sin through ignorance, in the holy things of the Lord; then he shall bring for his trespass unto the Lord a ram without blemish out of the flocks, with your estimation by shekels of silver, after the shekel of the sanctuary, for a trespass offering: And he shall make amends for the harm that he has done in the holy thing, and shall add the fifth part thereto, and give it unto the priest: and the priest shall make an atonement for him with the ram of the trespass offering, and it shall be forgiven him" (Lev 5:15-16). And again we read, "And if you

have erred, and not observed all these commandments, which the Lord has spoken unto Moses, even all that the Lord has commanded you by the hand of Moses, from the day that the Lord commanded Moses, and henceforward among your generations; Then it shall be, if ought be committed by ignorance without the knowledge of the congregation, that all the congregation shall offer one young bullock for a burnt offering, for a sweet savor unto the Lord, with his meat offering, and his drink offering, according to the manner, and one kid of the goats for a sin offering. And the priest shall make an atonement for all the congregation of the children of Israel, and it shall be, forgiven them for it is ignorance: and they shall bring their offering, a sacrifice made by fire unto the Lord, and their sin offering before the Lord, for their ignorance" (Num 15:22-25). It is in view of such Scriptures as these that we find David prayed, "Cleanse you me from secret faults" (Psalm 19:12).

Sin is always sin in the sight of God whether we are conscious of it or not. Sins of ignorance need atonement just as truly as do conscious sins. God is holy, and He will not lower His standard of righteousness to the level of our ignorance. Ignorance is not innocence. As a matter of fact, ignorance is more culpable now than it was in the days of Moses. We have no excuse for our ignorance.

God has clearly and fully revealed His will. The Bible is in our hands, and we cannot plead ignorance of its contents except to condemn our laziness. God has spoken, and by His Word we shall be judged.

And yet the fact remains that we are ignorant of many things, and the fault and blame are ours. And this does not minimize the enormity of our guilt. Sins of ignorance need divine forgiveness, as our Lord's prayer here plainly shows. Learn then how high is God's standard, how great is our need, and praise Him for an atonement of infinite sufficiency, which cleanses from all sin.

"Then said Jesus, Father, forgive them for they know not what they do."

4. Here we see the blindness of the human heart. "They know not what they do." This does not mean that the enemies of Christ were ignorant of the fact of His crucifixion. They did know full well that they had cried out "Crucify him." They did know full well that their vile request had been granted them by Pilate. They did know full well that He had been nailed to the tree, for they were eyewitnesses of the crime. What then did our Lord mean when He said, "They know not what they do?" He meant they were ignorant of the enormity of their crime. They "knew not" that it was the Lord of Glory they were crucifying. The emphasis is not on "they know not," but on "they know not what they do."

And yet they ought to have known. Their blindness was inexcusable. The Old Testament prophecies which had received their fulfilment in Him were sufficiently plain to identify Him as the Holy One of God. His teaching was unique, for His very critics were forced to admit "Never man spoke like this man" (John 7:46). And what of His perfect life! He had lived before men a life which had never been lived on earth before. He pleased not Himself. He went about doing good. He was ever at the disposal of others. There was no self-seeking about Him. His was a life of self-sacrifice from beginning to end. His was a life ever lived to the glory of God. His was a life on which was stamped Heaven's approval, for the Father's voice testified audibly "This is my beloved son, in whom I am well pleased." No, there was no excuse for their ignorance. It only demonstrated the blindness of their hearts. Their rejection of the Son of God bore full witness, once for all, that the carnal mind is "enmity against God."

How sad to think this terrible tragedy is still being repeated! Sinner, you little know what you are doing in neglecting God's great salvation. You little know how awful is the sin of slighting the Christ of God and spurning the invitations of His mercy. You little know the deep guilt which is attached to your act of refusing to receive the only One who can save you from your sins. You little know how fearful is the crime of saying, "We will not have this man reign over us." You know not what you do. You regard the vital issue with callous indifference. The question comes today as it did of old, "What shall I do with Jesus which is called Christ?" for you have to do something with Him: either you despise and reject Him, or you receive Him as the Savior of your soul and the Lord of your life.

But I say again, it seems to you a matter of small moment, of little importance, which you do. For years you have resisted the striving of His Spirit. For years you have shelved the all-important consideration. For years you have steeled your heart against Him, closed your eyes to His appeals, and shut your eyes to His surpassing beauty. Ah! you know not what you do. You are blind to your madness. Blind to your terrible sin. Yet are you not excuseless. You may be saved now if you will. "Believe on the Lord Jesus Christ, and you shall be saved." O come to the Savior now and say with one of old, "Lord, that I might receive my sight."

"Then said Jesus, Father, forgive them, for they know not what they do."

5. Here we see a lovely exemplification of His own teaching. In the Sermon on the Mount our Lord taught His disciples "Love your enemies, bless them that curse you, do good to them that hate you, and pray for them which despitefully use you and persecute you" (Mat 5:44). Above all others, Christ practiced what He preached. Grace and truth came by Jesus Christ. He not only taught the truth but was Himself the truth incarnate. Said He, "I am the way, the truth and the life" (John 14:6). So here on the Cross He perfectly exemplified His teaching of the mount. In all things He has left us an example.

Notice Christ did not personally forgive His enemies. So, in Matthew 5:44 He did not exhort His disciples to forgive their enemies, but He does exhort them to "pray" for them. But are we not to forgive those who wrong us? This leads us to a point concerning which there is much need for instruction today. Does Scripture teach that under all circumstances we must always forgive? I answer emphatically, it does not. The Word of God says, "If your brother trespass against you, rebuke him; and if he repent, forgive him. And if he trespass against you seven times a day, and seven times in a day turn again to you saying, I repent; you shall forgive him" (Luke 17:3-4). Here we are plainly taught that a condition must be met by the offender before we may pronounce forgiveness. The one who has wronged us must first "repent," that is, judge himself for his wrong and give evidence of his sorrow over it.

But suppose the offender does not repent? Then I am not to forgive him. But let there be no misunderstanding of our meaning here. Even though the one who has wronged me does not repent, nevertheless, I must not harbour ill-feelings against him. There must be no hatred or malice cherished in the heart. Yet, on the other hand, I must not treat the offender as if he had done no wrong. That would be to condone the offense, and therefore I should fail to uphold the requirements of righteousness, and this the believer is ever to do. Does God ever forgive where there is no repentance? No, for Scripture declares, "If we confess our sins, he is faithful and just to forgive us our sins and to cleanse us from all unrighteousness" (1 John 1:9).

One thing more. If one has injured me and repented not, while I cannot forgive him and treat him as though he had not offended, nevertheless, not only must I hold no malice in my heart against him, but I must also pray for him. Here is the value of Christ's perfect example. If we cannot forgive, we can pray for God to forgive him.

"Then said Jesus, Father, forgive them, for they know not what they do."

6. Here we see man's great and primary need. The first important lesson which all need to learn is that we are sinners, and as such, unfit for the presence of a Holy God. It is in vain that we select noble ideals, form good resolutions, and adopt excellent rules to live by, until the sin-question has been settled. It is of no avail that we attempt to develop a beautiful character and aim to do that which

will meet God's approval while there is sin between Him and our souls. Of what use are shoes if our feet are paralyzed. Of what use are glasses if we are blind. The question of the forgiveness of my sins is basic, fundamental, vital. It matters not that I am highly respected by a wide circle of friends if I am yet in my sins. It matters not that I have made good in business if I am an unpardoned transgressor in the sight of God. What will matter most in the hour of death is: Have my sins been put away by the blood of Christ?

The second all-important lesson which all need to learn is how forgiveness of sins may be obtained. What is the ground on which a Holy God will forgive sins? And here it is important to remark that there is a vital difference between divine forgiveness and much of human forgiveness. As a general rule, human forgiveness is a matter of leniency, often of laxity. We mean forgiveness is shown at the expense of justice and righteousness. In a human court of law, the judge has to choose between two alternatives: when the one in the dock has been proven guilty, the judge must either enforce the penalty of the law, or he must disregard the requirements of the law —the one is justice, the other is mercy. The only possible way by which the judge can both enforce the requirements of the law and yet

show mercy to its offender, is by a third party offering to suffer in his own person the penalty which the convicted one deserves. Thus, it was in the divine counsels. God would not exercise mercy at the expense of justice. God, as the Judge of all the earth, would not set aside the demands of His holy Law. Yet, God would show mercy. How? through One making full satisfaction to His outraged Law. Through His own Son taking the place of all those who believe on Him and bearing their sins in His own body on the tree. God could be just and yet merciful, merciful, and yet just. Thus, it is that "grace reigns through righteousness."

A righteous ground has been provided on which God can be just and yet the justifier of all who believe. Hence it is we are told, "Thus it is written, and thus it behooved Christ to suffer, and to rise from the dead the third day; And that repentance and remission (forgiveness) of sin should be preached in his name among all nations, beginning at Jerusalem" (Luke 24:46-47). And again, "Be it known unto you therefore, men and brethren, that through this man is preached unto your forgiveness of sins: And by him all that believe are justified from all things, from which you could not be justified by the Law of Moses" (Act 13:38-39). It was in view of the blood He was shedding that the Savior cried, "Father, forgive them." It was in view of the atoning sacrifice He was offering, that it can be said, "without shedding of blood is no remission."

In praying for the forgiveness of His enemies, Christ struck right down to the root of their need. And their need was the need of every child of Adam. Reader, have your sins been forgiven? that is, remitted or sent away? Are you, by grace, one of those of whom it is said, "In whom we have redemption through his blood, even the forgiveness of sins" (Col 1:4)?

"Then said Jesus, Father, forgive them, for they know not what they do."

7. Here we see the triumph of redeeming love. Mark closely the word with which our text opens: "Then." The verse which immediately precedes it reads thus, "And when they were come to the place, which is called Calvary, there they crucified him, and the malefactors, one on the right hand and the other on the left." "Then, said Jesus, Father, forgive them." Then, when man had done his worst. Then, when the vileness of the human heart was displayed in climactic devilry. Then, when with wicked hands the creature had dared to crucify the Lord of Glory. He might have uttered awful maledictions over them. He might have let loose the thunderbolts of righteous wrath and slain them. He might have caused the earth to open her mouth so that they had gone down alive into the pit. But no. Though subjected to unspeakable shame, though suffering excruciating pain, though despised, rejected, hated, nevertheless, He cries, "Father, forgive

them." That was the triumph of redeeming love. "Love suffers long and is kind...bears all things...endures all things" (1 Corinthians 13). Thus, it was shown at the Cross.

When Samson came to his dying hour, he used his great strength of body to encompass the destruction of his foes; but the Perfect One exhibited the strength of His love by praying for the forgiveness of His enemies. Matchless grace! "Matchless," we say, for even Stephen failed to fully follow the blessed example set by the Savior. If the reader will turn to Acts 7, he will find that Stephen's first thought was of himself, and then he prayed for his enemies "And they stoned Stephen, calling upon God, and saying, Lord Jesus receive my spirit. And he kneeled down and cried with a loud voice, Lord, lay not this sin to their charge" (Act 7:59-60). But with Christ the order was reversed: He prayed first for His foes, and last for Himself. In all things He has the pre-eminence.

Application And now one concluding word of application and exhortation. Should this chapter have been read by an unsaved person we would earnestly ask him to weigh well the next sentence. How dreadful must it be to oppose Christ and His truth knowingly! Those who crucified the Savior "knew not what they did." But, my reader, there is a very real and solemn sense in which this is not true of you. You know you ought to receive Christ as your Savior, that you ought to crown Him the Lord of your life, that you ought to make it your first and last concern to please and glorify Him. Be warned then; your danger is great. If you deliberately turn from Him, you turn from the only One who can save you from your sins, and it is written, "If we sin wilfully after that we have received the knowledge of the truth, there remains no more sacrifice for sins. But a certain fearful looking for of judgment and of fiery indignation, which shall devour the adversaries" (Heb 10:26-27).

It only remains for us to add a word on the blessed completeness of divine forgiveness. Many of God's people are unsettled and troubled upon this point. They understand how that all the sins they committed before they received Christ as their Savior have been forgiven, but oftentimes they are not clear concerning the sins which they commit after they have been born again. Many suppose it is possible for them to sin away the pardon which God has bestowed upon them. They suppose that the blood of Christ dealt with their past only, and that so far as the present and the future are concerned, they have to take care of that themselves. But of what value would be a pardon which might be taken away from me at any time? Surely there can be no settled peace when my acceptance with God and my going to Heaven is made to depend upon my holding on to Christ, or my obedience and faithfulness.

Blessed be God, the forgiveness which He bestows covers all sins past, present and future. Fellow-believer, did not Christ bear your "sins" in His own body on the tree? And were not all your sins future sins when He died? Surely, for at that time you had not been born, and so had not committed a single sin. Very well then: Christ bore your "future" sins as truly as your past ones. What the Word of God teaches is that the unbelieving soul is brought out of the place of unforgiveness into the place to which forgiveness attaches. Christians are a forgiven people. Says the Holy Spirit: "Blessed is the man to whom the Lord will not impute sin" (Rom 4:8)! The believer is in Christ, and their sin will never again be imputed to us. This is our place or position before God. In Christ is where He beholds us. And because I am in Christ I am completely and eternally forgiven, so much so that never again will sin be laid to my charge as touching my salvation, even though I were to remain on earth a hundred years. I am out of that place for evermore. Listen to the testimony of Scripture: "And you being dead in your sins and the uncircumcision of your flesh, has he (God) quickened together with him (Christ), having forgiven you all trespasses" (Col 2:13). Mark the two things which are here united (and what God has joined together let not man put asunder) my union with a risen Christ is connected with my forgiveness!

If then my life is "hid with Christ in God" (Col 3:3), then I am forever out of the place where imputation of sin applies. Hence it is written, "There is therefore now no condemnation to them which are in Christ Jesus" (Rom 8:1) how could there be if "all trespasses" have been forgiven? None can lay anything to the charge of God's elect (Rom 8:33). Christian reader, join the writer in praising God because we are eternally forgiven everything.

2. The Word Of Salvation

"And he said unto Jesus, Lord, remember me when you come into your kingdom. And Jesus said unto him, Truly I say unto you, Today shall you be with me in paradise." Luke 23:42-43

The second of Christ's cross-utterances was spoken in response to the request of the dying thief. Before considering the words of the Savior, we shall first ponder what occasioned them.

It was no accident that the Lord of Glory was crucified between two thieves. There are no accidents in a world that is governed by God. Much less could there have been any accident on that day of all days, or in connection with that event of all events, a day and an event which lie at the very centre of the world's history. No; God was presiding over that scene. From all eternity He had decreed when and where and how and with whom His Son should die. Nothing was left to chance or the caprice of man. All that God had decreed came to pass exactly as He had ordained, and nothing happened save as He had eternally purposed. Whatever man did was simply that which God's hand and counsel "determined to be done" (Act 4:28).

When Pilate gave orders that the Lord Jesus should be crucified between the two malefactors, all unknown to himself, he was but putting into execution the eternal decree of God and fulfilling His prophetic word. Seven hundred years before this Roman officer gave his command, God had declared through Isaiah that His Son should be "numbered with the transgressors" (Isa 53:12). How utterly unlikely this appeared, that the Holy One of God should be numbered with the unholy; that the very One whose finger had inscribed on the tables of stone the Sinaitic Law, should be assigned a place with the lawless; that the Son of God should be executed with criminals—this seemed utterly inconceivable. Yet it actually came to pass. Not a single word of God can fall to the ground. "Forever, O Lord, your word is settled in Heaven" (Psalm 119:89). Just as God had ordained, and just as He had announced, so it came to pass.

Why did God order it that His beloved Son should be crucified between two criminals? Certainly, God had a reason; a good one, a manifold one, whether we can discern it or not. God never acts arbitrarily. He has a good purpose for everything He does, for all His works are ordered by infinite wisdom. In this particular instance a number of answers suggest themselves to our inquiry. Was not our blessed Lord crucified with the two thieves to fully demonstrate the unfathomable depths of shame into which He had descended? At His birth He was surrounded by the beasts of the field, and now, at His death, He is numbered with the refuse of humanity. Again, was not the Savior numbered with transgressors to show us the position He occupied as our substitute? He had taken the place which was due us, and what was that but the place of shame, the place of transgressors, the place of criminals condemned to death! Again, was He not deliberately humiliated thus by Pilate to exhibit man's estimate of the peerless One "despised" as well as rejected! Again, was He not crucified with the two thieves, so that in those three crosses and the ones who hung upon them we might have a vivid and concrete representation of the drama of Salvation and man's response thereto the Savior's redemption, the sinner repenting and believing, and the sinner reviling and rejecting?

2 It should be added by way of explanation, that it is the judicial aspect we have dealt with. Restorative forgiveness which is the bringing back again into communion of a sinning believer dealt with

in 1 John 1:9 is another matter altogether.

Another important lesson which we may learn from the crucifixion of Christ between the two thieves, and the fact that one received Him and the other rejected Him, is that of the Sovereignty of God. The two malefactors were crucified together. They were equally near to Christ. Both of them saw and heard all that transpired during those fateful six hours. Both were notoriously wicked; both were suffering acutely; both were dying; and both urgently needed forgiveness. Yet one of them died in his sins, died as he had lived hardened and impenitent; while the other repented of his wickedness, believed in Christ, called on Him for mercy, and went to Paradise. How can this be accounted for except by the sovereignty of God! We see precisely the same thing going on today. Under exactly the same circumstances and conditions, one is melted, and another remains unmoved. Under the same sermon one man will listen with indifference, while another will have his eyes opened to see his need, and his will moved, to close with God's offer of mercy. To one the Gospel is revealed, to another it is "hidden." Why? All we can say is, "Even so Father, for so it seemed good in your sight" (Mat 11:26)

And yet God's sovereignty is never meant to destroy human responsibility. Both are plainly taught in the Bible, and it is our business to believe and preach both, whether we can harmonize or understand them or not. In preaching we may seem to our hearers to contradict ourselves, but what matters that? Said the late C.H. Spurgeon, when preaching on 1 Timothy 2:3-4, "There stands the text, and I believe that it is my Father's wish that 'all men should be saved and come to the knowledge of the truth.' But I know, also, that He does not will it, so that He will save any one of them, unless they believe in His Son; for He has told us over and over again that He will not. He will not save any man except he forsake his sins and turns to Him with full purpose of heart: that I also know. And I know, also, that He has a people whom He will save, whom by His eternal love He has chosen and whom by His eternal power He will deliver. I do not know how that square with this, that is another of the things I do not know." And said this prince of preachers, "I will just stand to what I ever shall and always have preached, and take God's Word as it stands, whether I can reconcile it with another part of God's Word or not."

We say again, God's sovereignty is never meant to destroy man's responsibility. We are to make diligent use of all the means which God has appointed for the salvation of souls. We are bidden to preach the Gospel to "every creature." Grace is free; the invitation is broad enough to take in "whoever believes." Christ turns away none who come to Him. Yet, after we have done all, after we have planted and watered, it is God who "gives the increase," and this He does as best pleases His sovereign will.

In the salvation of the dying thief, we have a clear view of victorious grace, such as is to be found nowhere else in the Bible. God is the God of all grace, and salvation is entirely by His grace. "By grace are you saved" (Eph 2:8), and it is "by grace" from beginning to end. Grace planned salvation, grace provided salvation, and grace so works on and in His elect as to overcome the hardness of their hearts, the obstinacy of their wills, and the enmity of their minds, and thus makes them willing to receive salvation. Grace begins, grace continues, and grace consummates our salvation.

Salvation by grace sovereign, irresistible, free grace is illustrated in the New Testament by example as well as precept. Perhaps the two most striking cases of all are those of Saul of Tarsus and the dying robber. And the case of the latter is even more noteworthy than the former. In the case of Saul, who afterwards became Paul the apostle to the Gentiles, there was an exemplary moral character to begin with. Writing years afterwards of his condition before his conversion, the apostle declared that as touching the righteousness of the Law he was "blameless" (Phi 3:6). He was a "Pharisee of the Pharisees": punctilious in his habits, correct in his deportment. Morally, his character was flawless. After his conversion his life was one of Gospel righteousness. Constrained by the love of Christ he spent himself in preaching the Gospel to sinners and in labouring to build up the saints. Doubtless our readers will agree with us when we say that probably Paul came nearest to attaining the ideals of the Christian life, and that he followed after his Master more closely than any other saint has since.

But with the saved thief it was far otherwise. He had no normal life before his conversion and no life of active service after it. Before his conversion he respected neither the Law of God nor the law of man. After his conversion he died without having opportunity to engage in the service of Christ. I would emphasize this, because these are the two things which are regarded by so many as contributing factors to our salvation. It is supposed that we must first fit ourselves by developing a noble character before God will receive us as His sons; and that after He has received us, tentatively, we are merely placed on probation, and that unless we now bring forth a certain quality and quantity of good works we shall "fall from grace and be lost." But the dying thief had no good works either before or after conversion. Hence, we are shut up to the conclusion that if saved at all he was certainly saved by sovereign grace.

The salvation of the dying thief also disposes of another prop which the legality of the carnal mind interposes to rob God of the glory due unto His grace. Instead of attributing the salvation of lost sinners to the matchless grace of God, many professing Christians seek to account for them by human influences, instrumentalities, and circumstances. Either the preacher, or providential and propitious circumstances, or the prayers of believers, are looked to as the main cause. Let us not be misunderstood here. It is true that often God is pleased to use means in the conversion of sinners; that frequently He condescends to bless our prayers and efforts to point sinners to Christ; that many times He causes His providences to awaken and arouse the ungodly to a realization of their state. But God is not shut up to these things. He is not limited to human instrumentalities.

His grace is all powerful, and when He pleases, that grace is able to save in spite of the lack of human instrumentalities, and in the face of unfavourable circumstances. So, it was in the case of the saved thief. Consider his conversion occurred at a time when to outward appearance Christ had lost all power to save either Himself or others. This thief had marched along with the Savior through the streets of Jerusalem and had seen Him sink beneath the weight of the Cross! It is highly probable that, as one who followed the occupation of a thief and robber, this was the first day he had ever set eyes on the Lord Jesus; and now that he did see Him, it was under every circumstance of weakness and disgrace. His enemies were triumphing over Him. His friends had mostly forsaken Him. Public opinion was unanimously against Him. His very crucifixion was regarded as utterly inconsistent with His Messiahship. His lowly condition was a stumbling-block to the Jews from the very first, and the circumstances of His death must have intensified it, especially to one who had never seen Him except in this condition. Even those who had believed on Him were made to doubt by His crucifixion. There was not one in the crowd who stood there without stretched finger and cried, "Behold the Lamb of God which takes away the sin of the world"! And yet, notwithstanding these obstacles and difficulties in the way of his faith, the thief apprehended the Saviorhood and Lordship of Christ. How can we possibly account for such faith and such spiritual understanding in one circumstanced as he was? How can we explain the fact that this dying thief took a suffering, bleeding, crucified man for his God! It cannot be accounted for apart from divine intervention and supernatural operation. His faith in Christ was a miracle of grace!

It is also to be remarked that the thief's conversion took place before the supernatural phenomena of that day. He cried, "Lord, remember me" before the hours of darkness, before the triumphant cry, "It is finished," before the rending of the temple veil before the quaking of the earth and the shivering of the rocks before the centurion's confession "Truly this was the Son of God." God purposely set his conversion before these things so that His sovereign grace might be magnified, and His sovereign power acknowledged. God designedly chose to save this thief under the most unfavourable circumstances that no flesh should glory in His presence. God deliberately arranged this combination of un-propitious conditions and surroundings to teach us that "Salvation is of the Lord," to teach us not to magnify human instrumentality above divine agency, to teach us that every genuine conversion is the direct product of the supernatural operation of the Holy Spirit.

We shall now consider together the thief himself, his various utterances, his request of the Savior, and our Lord's response "And he said unto Jesus, Lord, remember me when you come into your kingdom. And Jesus said unto him, Truly I say unto you, Today shall you be with me in paradise" (Luke 23:42-43).

1. Here we see a representative sinner. We shall never get to the heart of this incident until we regard the conversion of this man as a representative case, and the thief himself as a representative character. There are those who have sought to show that the original character of the repenting thief was nobler and worthier than that of the other who repented not. But this is not only not true to the facts of the case, but it serves to efface the peculiar glory of his conversion and takes away the wonderment of God's grace. It is of great importance to see that prior to the time when the one repented and believed there was no essential difference between the two thieves. In nature, in history, in circumstances they were one. The Holy Spirit has been careful to tell us that they both reviled the suffering Savior: "The chief priest mocking, with the scribes and elders said, he saved others; himself he cannot save. If he be the King of Israel, let him now come down from the Cross, and we will believe him. He trusted in God; let him deliver him now, if he will have him: for he said, I am the Son of God. The thieves also, which were crucified with him, cast the same in his teeth" (Mat 27:41-44).

Terrible indeed was the condition and action of this robber. On the very brink of eternity, he unites with the enemies of Christ in the awful sin of mocking Him. This was unparalleled turpitude. Think of it—a man in his dying hour deriding the suffering, Savior! O what a demonstration of human depravity and of the native enmity of the carnal mind against God! And reader, by nature there is the same depravity inherent within you, and unless a miracle of divine grace has been wrought upon you, there is the same enmity against God and His Christ present in your heart. You may not think so, you may not feel so, you may not believe so. But that does not alter the fact. The Word of Him who cannot lie declares, "The heart is deceitful above all things, and desperately wicked" (Jer 17:9). That is a statement of universal application. It describes what every human heart is by natural birth. And again, the same Scripture of truth declares, "The carnal mind is enmity against God: for it is not subject to the Law of God, neither indeed can be" (Rom 8:7). This, too, diagnoses the state of every descendant of Adam. "For there is no difference: for all have sinned and come short of the glory of God" (Rom 3:22-23). Unspeakably solemn is this: yet it needs to be pressed. It is not until our desperate condition is realized that we discover our need of a divine Savior. It is not until we are brought to see our total corruption and unsoundness that we shall hasten to the great Physician. It is not until we find in this dying thief a portrayal of ourselves that we shall join in saying, "Lord, remember me."

We have to be abased before we can be exalted. We have to be stripped of the filthy rags of our self-righteousness before we are ready for the garments of salvation. We have to come to God as beggars, empty-handed, before we can receive the gift of eternal life. We have to take the place of lost sinners before Him if we would be saved. Yes, we have to acknowledge ourselves as thieves before we can have a place in the family of God.

"But," you say, "I am no thief! I acknowledge I am not all I ought to be. I am not perfect. In fact, I will go so far as to admit I am a sinner. But I cannot allow that this thief represents my state and condition." Ah, friend, your case is far worse than you suppose. You are a thief, and that of the worst type. You have robbed God! Suppose that a firm in the East appointed an agent to represent them in the West, and that every month they forwarded to him his salary. But suppose also at the end of the year his employers discovered that, though the agent had been cashing the checks they sent him, nevertheless, he had served another firm all that time. Would not that agent be a thief? Yet this is precisely the situation and state of every sinner. He has been sent into this world by God, and God has endowed him with talents and the capacity to use and improve them. God has blessed him with health and strength; He has supplied his every need and provided innumerable opportunities to serve and glorify Him. But with what result? The very things God has given him have been misappropriated. The sinner has served another master, even Satan. He dissipates his strength and wastes his time in the pleasures of sin. He has robbed God. Unsaved reader, in the sight of Heaven your condition is as desperate, and your heart is as wicked as that of the thief. See in him a picture of yourself!

2. Here we see that man has to come to the end of himself before he can be saved. Above we have contemplated this dying robber as a representative sinner, a sample specimen of what all men are by nature and practice by nature at enmity against God and His Christ; by practice robbers of God, misusing what He has given us and failing to render what is due Him. We are now to see that this crucified robber was also a representative case in his conversion. And at this point we shall dwell simply upon his helplessness.

To see ourselves as lost sinners is not sufficient. To learn that we are corrupt and depraved by nature and sinful transgressors by practice is the first important lesson. The next is to learn that we are utterly undone, and that we can do nothing whatever to help ourselves. To discover that our condition is so desperate that it is entirely beyond human repair is the second step toward salvation looking at it from the human side. But if man is slow to learn that he is a lost sinner and unfit for the presence of a holy God, he is slower still to recognize that he can do nothing towards his salvation and is unable to work any improvement in himself so as to be fit for God. Yet, it is not until we realize that we are "without strength" (Rom 5:6), that we are "impotent," that it is not by works of righteousness which we do, but by His mercy God saves us (Ti 3:5), not until then shall we despair of ourselves, and look outside of ourselves to the One who can save us.

The great Scripture type of sin is leprosy, and for leprosy man can devise no cure. God alone can deal with this dreadful disease. So, it is with sin. But, as we have said, man is slow to learn his lesson. He is like the prodigal son, who when he had squandered his substance in the far country in riotous living and began to be "in want," instead of returning to the Father straightaway, he "went and joined himself to a citizen of that country" and went to the fields to feed swine in other words he went to work. Likewise, the sinner who has been aroused to his need, instead of going at once to Christ, he tries to work himself into God's favour. But he will fare no better than the prodigal, the husks of the swine will be his only portion. Or again, like the woman bowed down with her infirmity for many long years. She tried many physicians before she sought the great Physician: so, the awakened sinner seeks relief and peace in first one thing and then another, until he completes the weary round of religious performances, and ends by being "nothing bettered, but rather grows worse" (Mar 5:26). No; it is not until that woman had "spent all she had" that she sought Christ: and it is not until the sinner comes to the end of his own resources that he will betake himself to the Savior.

Before any sinner can be saved, he must come to the place of realized weakness. This is what the conversion of the dying thief shows us. What could he do? He could not walk in the paths of righteousness for there was a nail through either foot. He could not perform any good works for there was a nail through either hand. He could not turn over a new leaf and live a better life for he was dying. And, my reader, those hands of yours which are so ready for self-righteous acting, and those feet of yours which are so swift to run in the way of legal obedience, must be nailed to the Cross. The sinner has to be cut off from his own workings and be made willing to be saved by Christ. A realization of your sinful condition, of your lost condition, of your helpless condition, is nothing more or less than old-fashioned conviction of sin, and this is the sole prerequisite for coming to Christ for salvation, for Christ Jesus came into the world to save sinners.

3. Here we see the meaning of repentance and faith. Repentance may be considered under various aspects. It includes in its meaning and scope a change of mind about sin, a sorrowing for sin, a forsaking of sin. Yet there is more in repentance than these. Really, repentance is the realization of our lost condition, it is the discovery of our ruin, it is the judging of ourselves, it is the owning of our lost estate. Repentance is not so much an intellectual process as it is the conscience active in the presence of God. And this is exactly what we find here in the case of the thief. First, he says to his companion, "Do not you fear God, seeing you are in the same condemnation?" (Luke 23:40). A short time before he had mingled his voice with those who were reviling the Savior. But the Holy Spirit had been at work upon him, and now his conscience is active in the presence of God. It was not, "Do not you fear punishment?" But "Do not you fear God?" He apprehends God as Judge. And then, in the second place he adds, "And we are indeed justly; for we receive the due reward of our deeds" (Luke 23:41). Here we see him acknowledging his guilt and the justice of his condemnation. He passes sentence upon himself. He makes no excuses and attempts no extenuation. He recognized he was a transgressor, and that as such he fully deserved punishment for his sins, yes, that death was his due. Have you taken this position before God, my reader?

Have you openly confessed your sins to Him? Have you passed judgment upon yourself and your ways? Are you ready to acknowledge that death is your "due?" While ever you palliate sin or prevaricate about it, you are shutting yourself out from Christ. Christ came into the world to save sinners self-confessed sinners, sinners who really take the place of sinners before God, sinners who are conscious that they are lost and undone.

The thief's "repentance toward God" was accompanied with "faith toward our Lord Jesus Christ." In contemplating his faith, we may notice first that it was an intelligent head faith. In the earlier paragraphs of this chapter, we have called attention to the Sovereignty of God and His irresistible and victorious grace which were exhibited in the conversion of this thief. Now we turn to another side of the truth, equally necessary to press, a side which is not contradictory to what we have said previously, but rather, complementary, and supplementary.

Scripture does not teach that if God has elected a certain soul to be saved that that person will be saved whether they believe or not. That is a false conclusion drawn by those who reject the truth. No; Scripture teaches that the same God who predestined the end also predestined the means. The God who decreed the salvation of the dying thief fulfilled His decree by giving him a faith with which to believe. This is the plain teaching of 2 Thessalonians 2:13 and other Scriptures "God has from the beginning chosen you to salvation through sanctification of the Spirit and belief of the truth." This is just what we see here in connection with this robber. He "believed the truth." His faith took hold of the Word of God.

Over the Cross was the superscription, "This is Jesus the King of the Jews." Pilate had placed it there in derision. But it was the truth nevertheless, and after he had written it, God would not allow him to alter it. The board bearing this superscription had been carried in front of Christ through the streets of Jerusalem and out to the place of crucifixion, and the thief had read it, and divine grace and power had opened the eyes of his understanding to see that it was the truth. His faith grasped the Kingship of Christ, hence his mention of "when you come into your kingdom." Faith always rests on the written Word of God.

Before a man will believe that Jesus is the Christ, he must have the testimony before him that He is the Christ. Distinction is often made between head faith and heart faith, and properly so, for the distinction is real, and vital. Sometimes head faith is decried as valueless, but this is foolish. There must be head faith before there can be heart faith. We must believe intellectually before we can believe savingly in the Lord Jesus. Proof of this is seen in connection with the heathen: they have no head faith and therefore they have no heart faith. We readily grant that head faith will not save unless it is accompanied by heart faith, but we insist that there is no heart faith unless there has first been head faith. How can they believe in Him of whom they have not heard? True, one may believe about Him without believing (trusting) in Him, but one cannot believe in Him without first believing about Him. So, it was with the dying thief. In all probability he had never seen Christ before this day of his death, but he had seen the written superscription testifying to His Kingship, and the Holy Spirit used this as the basis of his faith. We say then that his was an intelligent faith: first an intellectual faith, the believing the written testimony submitted to him; second, a heart faith, the resting in confidence on Christ Himself as the Savior of sinners.

Yes, this dying robber exercised a heart faith which rested savingly on Christ. We shall try to be very simple here. A man may have head faith in the Lord Jesus and be lost. A man may believe about the historic Christ and be no better for it, just as he is no better for believing about the historic Napoleon. Reader, you may believe all about the Savior His perfect life, His sacrificial death, His victorious resurrection, His glorious ascension, His promised return but you must do more than this. Gospel faith is a confiding faith. Saving faith is more than a correct opinion or a train of reasoning. Saving faith transcends all reason.

Look at this dying thief! Was it reasonable that Christ should notice him? a crucified robber, a self-confessed criminal, one who a few minutes ago had been reviling Him! Was it reasonable that the Savior should take any notice of him? Was it reasonable to expect that he should be transported from the very brink of the Pit into Paradise? Ah, my reader, the head reasons, but the heart does not. And this man's petition came from his heart. He had not the use of his hands and feet (and they are not needed for salvation: they rather impede), but he had the use of his heart and tongue. They were free to believe and confess "with the heart man believes unto righteousness; and with the mouth confession is made unto salvation" (Rom 10:10).

We may also notice this was a humble faith. He prayed with becoming modesty. It was not "Lord, honour me," or "Lord, exalt me," but Lord, if You will but think of me! if You will only look on me "Lord, remember me." And yet that word remember was wonderfully full and appropriate. He might have said, Pardon me, Save me, Bless me but "remember" included them all. An interest in Christ's heart will include an interest in all His benefits! Moreover, this word was well suited to the condition of the one who uttered it. He was an outcast from society who would remember him?! The public would think no more of him. His friends would be glad to forget him as having disgraced his family. But there is One with Whom he ventures to lodge this petition "Lord, remember me."

Finally, we may notice that this was a courageous faith. Perhaps this is not apparent at first sight, but a little consideration will make it plain. He who hung on the central Cross was the One on whom all eyes were turned and toward whom all the vile mockery of a vulgar mob was directed. Every faction of that crowd joined in jeering at the Savior. Matthew tells us that "they had passed by and reviled Him," that "likewise also the chief priests mocked, with the elders and scribes." While Luke informs us "the soldiers also mocked him" (23:36). It is therefore easy to understand why the thieves should also take up the taunting cry. No doubt the priests and the scribes smiled benignly upon them as they did so. But suddenly there was a change. The repenting thief instead of continuing to sneer and jibe at Christ, turns to his companion, and openly rebukes him in the hearing of the spectators gathered around the crosses, crying, "This man has done nothing amiss." Thus, he condemned the whole Jewish nation! But more; not only does he bear testimony to Christ's innocence, but he also confessed His Kingship. And thus, by a single stroke he cuts himself off from the favour of his companion and of the crowd as well! We talk today of the courage, which is needed to openly witness for Christ, but such a courage in these days' pales into utter insignificance before the courage displayed that day by the dying thief.

4. Here we see a marvellous case of spiritual illumination. It is perfectly wonderful the progress made by this man in those few dying hours. His growth in grace and in the knowledge of his Lord was amazing. From the brief record of the words that fell from his lips we may discover seven things which he had learned under the tuition of the Holy Spirit.

First, he expresses his belief in a future life where retribution would be meted out by a righteous and sin-avenging God. "Do not you fear God?" proves this. He sharply reprimands his companion, and as much as says, How dare you have the temerity to revile this innocent man? Remember, that shortly you will have to appear before God and face a tribunal infinitely more solemn than the one which sentenced you to be crucified. God is to be feared, so be silent.

Second, as we have seen, he had a sight of his own sinfulness "You are in the same condemnation. And we are indeed justly for we receive the due reward of our deeds" (Luke 23:40-41). He recognized that he was a transgressor. He saw that sin merited punishment, that "condemnation" was just. He owned that death was his "due." This was something that his companion neither confessed nor recognized.

Third, he bore testimony to Christ's sinlessness "This man has done nothing amiss" (Luke 23:41). And here we may mark the pains God took to guard the spotless character of His Son. Especially is this to be seen toward the end. Judas was moved to say, "I have betrayed innocent blood." Pilate testified, "I find no fault in him." Pilate's wife said, "Have nothing to do with this just man." And now that He hangs on the Cross, God opens the eyes of this robber to see the faultlessness of His beloved Son and opens his lips so that he bears witness to His excellency.

Fourth, he not only witnessed to the sinless humanity of Christ, but he also confessed His Godhead "Lord, remember me," he said. A marvellous word was that. The Savior nailed to the tree, the object of Jewish hatred and the butt of a vulgar mob's ridicule. This thief had heard the scornful challenge of the priests. "If you be the Son of God, come down from the cross" (Mat 27:40), and no response had been given. But moved by faith and not by sight, he recognizes and owns the deity of the central Sufferer.

Fifth, he believed in the Saviourhood of the Lord Jesus. He had heard Christ's prayer for His enemies, "Father, forgive them," and to one whose heart the Lord had opened, that short sentence became a saving sermon. His own cry, "Lord, remember me" included within its scope, "Lord, save me," which therefore implies his faith in the Lord Jesus as Savior. In fact, he must have believed that Jesus was a Savior for the chief of sinners or how could he have believed that Christ would "remember" such as he!

Sixth, he evidenced his faith in Christ's kingship "when you come into your kingdom." This too, was a wonderful word. Outward circumstances all seemed to belie His kingship. Instead of being seated on a throne, He hung upon a Cross. Instead of wearing a royal diadem, His brow was encircled with thorns. Instead of being waited upon by a retinue of servants, He was numbered with transgressors. Nevertheless, He was King, King of the Jews (Mat 2:2).

Finally, he looked forward to the Second Coming of Christ "when you come." He looked away from the present to the future. He saw beyond the "sufferings" the "glory." Over the Cross, the eye of faith detected the crown. And in this he was before the apostles, for unbelief had closed their eyes. Yes, he looked beyond the first advent in shame, to the Second Advent in power and majesty.

And how can we account for the spiritual intelligence of this dying robber? Whence did he receive such insight into the things of Christ? How comes it that this babe in Christ made such amazing progress in the school of God? It can be accounted for only by divine influence. The Holy Spirit was his Teacher! Flesh and blood had not revealed these things unto him but the Father in Heaven. What an illustration that divine things are hidden from "the wise and prudent" and are revealed to "babes"!

5. Here we see the Saviorhood of Christ. The crosses were only a few feet apart and it did not take the Savior long to hear this cry of the penitent thief. What was His response thereto? He might have said, You deserve your fate: you are a wicked robber and have merited death. Or, He might have replied, You have left it until too late: you should have sought Me sooner. Ah! but had He not promised, "Him that comes to me I will in no wise cast out!" So, it proved here.

Of the reproaches which were cast on Him by the crowd, the Lord Jesus took no notice. To the insulting challenge of the priests to descend from the Cross, He made no response. But the prayer of this contrite, believing thief arrested His attention. At the time He was grappling with the powers of darkness and sustaining the awful load of His people's guilt, and we should have thought He might be excused from attending to individual applications. Ah! but a sinner can never come to Christ in an unacceptable time. He gives him an answer of peace and that without delay.

The salvation of the repentant and believing robber illustrates not only Christ's readiness but also His power to save sinners. The Lord Jesus is no feeble Savior. Blessed be God, He is able to "save unto the uttermost" them that come unto God by Him. And never was this so signally displayed as when on the Cross. This was the time of the

Redeemer's "weakness" (2 Corinthians 13:4). When the thief cried "Lord, remember me," the Savior was in agony on the accursed tree. Yet even then, even there, He had power to redeem this soul from death and open for him the gates of Paradise! Never doubt then or question the infinite sufficiency of the Savior. If a dying Savior could save, how much more He who rose in triumph from the tomb never more to die! In saving this thief, Christ gave an exhibition of His power at the very time when it was almost clouded.

The salvation of the dying thief demonstrates that the Lord is willing and able to save all who come to Him. If Christ received this penitent, believing thief, then none need despair of a welcome if they will but come to Christ. If this dying robber was not beyond the reach of divine mercy, then none are who will respond to the invitations of divine grace. The Son of Man came "to seek and to save that which was lost" (Luke 19:10), and none can sink lower than that. The Gospel of Christ is the power of God "to everyone that believes" (Rom 1:16). O limit not the grace of God. A Savior is provided for the very "chief of sinners" (1 Timothy 1:15), if only he will believe. Even those who reach the dying hour yet in their sins are not beyond hope. Personally, I believe that very, very few are saved on a deathbed, and it is the height of folly for any man to postpone his salvation until then, for there is no guarantee that any man will have a deathbed. Many are cut off suddenly, without any opportunity to lie down and die. Yet even one on a deathbed is not beyond the reach of divine mercy. As said one of the Puritans, "There is one such case recorded that none need despair, but only one, in Scripture, that none might presume."

Yes, here we see the Saviorhood of Christ. He came into this world to save sinners, and He left it and went to Paradise accompanied by a saved criminal, the first trophy of His redeeming blood!

6. Here we see the destination of the saved at death. In his splendid book The Seven Sayings of Christ on the Cross, Dr. Anderson-Berry has pointed out that the word "Today" is not correctly placed in the rendering of our King James Version, and that the designed

correspondence between the thief's request and Christ's response requires a different construction of the latter. The form of Christ's reply is evidently designed to match in its order of thought the robber's petition. This will be seen if we arrange the two in parallel couplets thus: And he said unto Jesus And Jesus said unto him, Truly I say unto you Lord, remember me You shall be with me when you come into Today in Paradise. your kingdom.

By arranging the words thus, we discover the correct emphasis. "Today" is the emphatic word. In our Lord's gracious response to the thief's request, we have a striking illustration of how divine grace exceeds human expectations. The thief prayed that the Lord would remember him in His coming Kingdom, but Christ assures him that before that very day had passed, he should be with the Savior. The thief asked to be remembered in an earthly kingdom, but Christ assured him of a place in Paradise. The thief simply asked to be "remembered," but the Savior declared he should be "with him." Thus does God exceedingly abundantly above all that we ask or think.

Not only does Christ's reply signify the survival of the soul after the death of the body, but it tells us that the believer is with Him during the interval which divides death from the resurrection. To make this more emphatic Christ prefaced His promise with the solemn but assuring words "Truly I say unto you." It was this prospect of going to Christ at death which cheered the martyr Stephen in his last hour and therefore did he cry "Lord Jesus receive my spirit" (Act 7:59). It was this blessed expectation which moved the apostle Paul to say, I have "a desire to depart and to be with Christ, which is far better" (Phi 1:23). Not unconsciousness in the grave, but with Christ in Paradise is what awaits every believer at death. Every "believer" I say, for the souls of unbelievers, instead of going to Paradise, pass to the place of torments, as is clear from our Lord's teaching in Luke 16. Reader, where would your soul go, if this moment you were dying?

How hard Satan has striven to hide this blessed prospect from the saints of God! On the one hand he has propagated the doleful dogma of soul-sleep, the teaching that believers are in a state of unconsciousness between death and the resurrection; and on the other hand, he has invented a horrible Purgatory, to terrify believers with the thought that at death they pass into fire, necessary to purify and fit them for Heaven. How thoroughly the word of Christ to the thief disposes of these God-dishonouring delusions! The thief went straight from the Cross to Paradise! The moment a sinner believes that moment is he "made meet to be a partaker of the inheritance of the saints in light" (Col 1:12). "For by one offering he has perfected forever them that are sanctified" (Heb 10:14). Our fitness for Christ's presence, as well as our title, rests solely on His shed blood.

7. Here we see the longing of the Savior for fellowship. In fellowship, we reach the climax of grace and the sum of Christian privilege. Higher than fellowship we cannot go. God has called us "unto the fellowship of his Son" (1 Corinthians 1:9). We are often told that we are "saved to serve," and this is true, but it is only a part of the truth and by no means the most wondrous and blessed part of it. We are saved for fellowship. God had innumerable "servants" before Christ came here to die, the angels ever do His bidding. Christ came not primarily to secure servants, but those who should enter into fellowship with Him.

That which makes Heaven superlatively attractive to the heart of a saint is not that Heaven is a place where we shall be delivered from all sorrow and suffering, nor is it that Heaven is the place where we shall meet again those we loved in the Lord, nor is it that Heaven is the place of golden streets and pearly gates and jasper walls no; blessed as these things are, Heaven without Christ would not be Heaven. It is Christ the heart of the believer longs for and pants after "Whom have I in Heaven but you? and there is none upon earth that I desire besides you" (Psalm 73:25). And the most amazing thing is that Heaven will not be Heaven to Christ in the highest sense until His redeemed are gathered around Him. It is His saints that His heart longs for. To come again and "receive us unto himself" is the joyous expectation set before Him. Not until He sees of the travail of His soul will He be fully satisfied. (Isa 53:11).

These are the thoughts suggested and confirmed by the words of the Lord Jesus to the dying thief. "Lord, remember me" had been his cry. And what was the response? Note it carefully. Had Christ merely said, "Truly I say unto you, Today you shall be in Paradise" that would have set at rest the fears of the thief. Yes, but it did not satisfy the Savior. That upon which His heart was set was the fact that that very day a soul saved by His precious blood should be with Him in Paradise! We say Again, this is the climax of grace and the sum of Christian blessing. Said the apostle, "I have a desire to depart and to be with Christ "(Phi 1:23). And again, he wrote, "Absent from the body" free from all pain and care? No. "Absent from the body" translated to glory? No. "Absent from the body...present with the Lord "(2 Corinthians 5:8). So, too, with Christ. Said He, "In my father's house are many mansions: if it were not so, I would have told you. I go to prepare a place for you."Yet, when He adds, "I will come again," He does not say "And conduct you unto the Father's house," or "I will take you to the place I have prepared for you," but "I will come again and receive you unto myself "(John 14:2-3). To be "forever with the Lord" (1 Thessalonians 4:17) is the goal of all our hopes; to have us forever with Himself is that to which He looks forward with eager and gladsome expectation.

"You shall be with me in Paradise!"

3. The Word Of Affection

"Now there stood by the cross of Jesus his mother. When Jesus therefore saw his mother, and the disciple standing by, whom he loved, he says unto his mother, Woman, behold your son! Then says he to the disciple, Behold your mother!" John 19:25a-26

"Now there stood by the cross of Jesus his mother" (John 19:25). Like her Son, Mary was not unacquainted with grief. At the beginning we are told, "And the angel came in unto her, and said, Hail, you are highly favoured, the Lord is with you; blessed are you among women. And when she saw him, she was troubled at his saying, and cast in her mind what manner of salutation this should be" (Luke 1:28-29). This was but the forerunner of many troubles: Gabriel had come to announce to her the fact of miraculous conception, and a moment's reflection will show us that it was no light matter for Mary to become the mother of our Lord in this mysterious and unheard-of way. It brought with it, no doubt, at a distant date, great honour but it brought with it for the present no small danger to Mary's reputation, and no small trial to her faith. It is beautiful to observe her quiet submission to the will of God "And Mary said, Behold the handmaid of the Lord; be it unto me according to your word" (Luke 1:38), was her response. This was lovely resignation. Nevertheless, she was "troubled" at the Annunciation and, as we have said, this was but the precursor of many trials and sorrows.

What sorrow it must have caused her when, because there was no room in the inn, she had to lay her newly born Babe in the manger! What anguish must have been hers when she learned of Herod's purpose to destroy her infant's life! What trouble was given her when she was forced on his account to flee into a foreign country and sojourn for several years in the land of Egypt! What piercings of soul must have been hers when she saw her Son despised and rejected of men! What grief must have wrung her heart as she beheld Him hated and persecuted by His own nation! And who can estimate what she passed through as she stood there at the Cross? If Christ was the Man of Sorrows, was she not the woman of sorrows?

"There stood by the cross of Jesus his mother."

1. Here we see the fulfilment of Simeon's prophecy. In accordance with the requirements of the Mosaic Law, the parents of the child Jesus brought Him to the Temple to present Him to the Lord. Then it was that old Simeon, who waited for the Consolation of Israel, took Him into his arms and blessed God. After saying, "Lord, now let your servant depart in peace, according to your word: for mine eyes have seen your salvation, which you have prepared before the face of all people; A light to lighten the Gentiles and the glory of your people Israel" (Luke 2:29-32) he now turned to Mary and said, "Behold, this child is set for the fall and rising again of many in Israel; and for a sign which shall be spoken against; (Yes, a sword shall pierce through your own soul also) that the thoughts of many hearts may be revealed" (Luke 2:34-35). A strange word was that! Could it be that hers, the greatest of all privileges was to bring with it the greatest of all sorrows? It seemed most unlikely at the time Simeon spoke. Yet how truly and how tragically did it come to pass! Here at the Cross was this prophecy of Simeon fulfilled.

"Now there stood by the Cross of Jesus his mother" (John 19:25). After the days of His infancy and childhood, and during all the public ministry of Christ, we see and hear so little of Mary. Her life was lived in the background, among the shadows. But now, when the supreme hour strikes of her Son's agony, when the world has cast out the child of her womb, she stands there by the Cross! Who can fitly portray such a picture? Mary was nearest to the cruel tree! Bereft of faith and hope, baffled, and paralyzed by the strange scene, yet bound with the golden chain of love to the dying One, there she stands! Try and read the thoughts and emotions of that mother's heart. O what a sword it was that pierced her soul then! Never such bliss at a human birth; never such sorrow at an inhuman death.

Here we see displayed the mother-heart. She is the dying man's mother. The One who agonizes there on the Cross is her child. She it was who first planted kisses on that brow now crowned with thorns. She it was who guided those hands and feet in their first infantile movements. No mother ever suffered as she did. His disciples may desert Him, His friends may forsake Him, His nation may despise Him, but His mother stands there at the foot of His Cross. Oh, who can fathom or analyse the mother-heart.

Who can measure those hours of sorrow and suffering as the sword was slowly drawn through Mary's soul! Hers was no hysterical or demonstrative sorrow. There was no show of feminine weakness; no wild outcry of uncontrollable anguish; no fainting. Not a word that fell from her lips has been recorded by any of the four evangelists: apparently, she suffered in unbroken silence. Yet her sorrow was none the less real and acute. Still waters run deep. She saw that brow pierced with cruel thorns, but she could not smooth it with her tender touch. She watched His pierced hands and feet grow numb and livid, but she might not chafe them. She marks His need of a drink, but she is not allowed to slake His thirst. She suffered in profound desolation of spirit.

"There stood by the cross of Jesus his mother" (John 19:25). The crowds are mocking, the thieves are taunting, the priests are jeering, the soldiers are callous and indifferent, the Savior is bleeding, dying and there is His mother beholding the horrible mockery. What wonder if she had swooned at such a sight! What wonder if she had turned away from such a spectacle! What wonder if she had fled from such a scene? But no! There she is, she does not crouch away, she does not faint, she does not even sink to the ground in her grief she stands. Her action and attitude are unique. In all the annals of the history of our race there is no parallel. What transcendent courage. She stood by the Cross of Jesus what marvellous fortitude. She represses her grief and stands there silent. Was it not reverence for the Lord which kept her from disturbing His last moments?

"When Jesus therefore saw his mother, and the disciple standing by whom he loved, he says unto his mother, Woman, behold your son, speaking of John. Then says he to the disciple, Behold your mother! And from that hour that disciple took her unto his own home" (John 19:26-27).

2. Here we see the perfect man setting an example for children to honour their parents. The Lord Jesus evidenced His perfection in the manner in which He fully discharged the obligations of every relationship that He sustained, either to God or man. On the Cross we behold His tender care and solicitude for His mother, and in this we have the pattern of Jesus Christ presented to all children for their imitation, teaching them how to acquit themselves toward their parents according to the laws of nature and grace.

The words which the Finger of God engraved on the two tables of stone, and which were given to Moses on Mount Sinai, have never been repealed. They are in force while the earth lasts. Each of them is embodied in the preceptive teaching of the New Testament. The words of Exodus 20:12 are reiterated in Ephesians 6:1-2 "Children, obey your parents in the Lord: for this is right. Honour your father and mother; which is the first commandment with promise; That it may be well with you, and you may live long on the earth."

The commandment for children to honour their parents goes far beyond a bare obedience to this expressed will, though, of course, it includes that. It embraces love and affection, gratitude, and respect. It is too often assumed that this fifth commandment is addressed to young folks only. Nothing can be further from the truth. Unquestionably it is addressed to children first, for in the order of nature children are always young first. But the conclusion that this commandment loses force when childhood is left behind is to miss at least half of its deep significance. As intimated, the word "honour" looks beyond obedience, though that is its first import. In the course of time the children grow to manhood and womanhood, which is the age of full personal responsibility, the age when they are no longer beneath the control of their parents yet has not their obligations to them ceased. They owe their parents a debt which they can never fully discharge. The very least they can do is to hold their parents in high esteem, to put them in the place of superiority to reverence them. In the perfect Exemplar we find both obedience and esteem manifested.

The fact that the last Adam came into this world not as did the first Adam in full possession of the distinguishing glories of humanity; fully developed in body and mind but as a babe, having to pass through the period of childhood, is a fact of tremendous importance and value in the light it casts on the fifth commandment. During His early years, the boy Jesus was under the control of Mary His mother and Joseph His legal father.

This is beautifully displayed in the second chapter of Luke. Arrived at the age of twelve, Jesus is taken by them to Jerusalem at the feast of the Passover. The picture presented is deeply suggestive if due attention is paid to it. At the close of the feast Joseph and Mary depart for Nazareth, accompanied by their friends and supposing that Jesus is with them. But, instead, He had remained behind in the royal city. After a day's journey, His absence is discovered. At once they turn back to Jerusalem, and there they find Him in the temple. His mother interrogates Him thus: "Son, why have you thus dealt with us? Behold, your father and I have sought you sorrowing" (Luke 2:48). The fact she had sought Him "sorrowing" strongly implies that He had hardly ever been outside the immediate sphere of her influence. Not to find Him at hand, was to her a new and strange experience, and the fact that she, assisted by Joseph, had sought Him "sorrowing" reveals the beautiful relationship existing between them in the home at Nazareth!

The answer that Jesus returned to her inquiry, when rightly understood, also reveals the honour in which He held His mother. We quite agree with Dr. Campbell Morgan (1863-1945) that Christ does not here rebuke her. It is largely a matter of finding the right emphasis "Knew you not?" As the afore-mentioned expositor well says, "It was as though He had said: 'Mother, surely you knew Me well enough to know that nothing could detain Me but the affairs of the Father.'"

The sequel is equally beautiful, for we read, "And he went down with them, and came to Nazareth, and was subject unto them" (Luke 2:51). And thus, for all time the Christ of God has set the example for children to obey their parents.

But more. As it is with us, so it was with Christ: the years of obedience to Mary and Joseph ended, but not so the years of "honour." In the last and awful hours of His human life, amid the infinite sufferings of the Cross, the Lord Jesus thought of her who loved Him and whom He loved; thought of her present necessity and provided for her future need by committing her to the care of that disciple who most deeply understood His love. His thought for Mary at that time and the honour He gave her was one of the manifestations of His victory over pain.

Perhaps a word is called for in connection with our Lord's form of address "Woman." So far as the record of the four Gospels go, never once did He call her "Mother." For us who live today, the reason for this is not hard to discern. Looking down the centuries with His omniscient foresight and seeing the awful system of Mariolatry so soon to be erected, He refrained from using a word which would in any wise countenance this idolatry, the idolatry of rendering to Mary the homage which is due alone to her Son; the idolatry of worshiping her as "The Mother of God."

Twice over in the Gospel records do we find our Lord addressing Mary as "Woman," and it is most noteworthy that both of these are found in John's Gospel, which, as is well known, sets forth our Savior's deity. The synoptics (Matthew, Mark, and Luke) set Him forth in human relationships; not so the fourth Gospel. John's Gospel presents Christ as the Son of God, and as Son of God He is above all human relationships, and hence the perfect consonance of presenting the Lord Jesus here addressing Mary as "Woman."

Our Lord's act on the Cross in commending Mary to the care of His beloved apostle is better understood in the light of His mother's widowhood. Though the Gospels do not specifically record his death, there is little doubt, but that Joseph died sometime before the Lord Jesus began His public ministry. Nothing is seen of Mary's husband after the incident recorded in Luke 2 when Christ was a boy of twelve. In John 2, Mary is seen at the marriage in Cana, but no hint is given that Joseph was present. It was in view, then, of Mary's widowhood, in view of the fact that the time had now arrived when He might no longer be a comfort to her by His bodily presence, that His loving care is manifested.

Permit just a brief word of exhortation. Probably these lines may be read by numbers of grownup people who still have living fathers and mothers. How are you treating them? Are you truly "honouring" them? Does this example of Christ on the Cross put you to shame? It maybe you are young and vigorous, and your parents Gray-headed and infirm; but says the Holy Spirit, "Despise not your mother when she is old" (Pro 23:22). It maybe you are rich, and they are poor; then fail not to make provision for them. It maybe they live in a distant state or land, then neglect not to write them words of appreciation and cheer which shall brighten their closing days. These are sacred duties. "Honour your father, and your mother."

3. Here we see that John had returned to the Savior's side. Excepting, of course, the suffering of Christ at the Hand of God, perhaps the bitterest dreg of all in the cup which He drank was the forsaking of Him by the apostles. It was bad enough and sad enough that His own people, the Jews, should despise and reject Him but it was far worse that the Eleven, who had companioned so long with Him, should desert their Lord in the hour of crisis. One would have thought that their faith and their love was equal to any shock. But it was not. "They all forsook him and fled" (Mat 26:56) reads the sacred narrative. Unspeakably tragic was this. Their failure to "watch" with Him for one hour in the garden well near paralyzes our minds, but their turning away from Him at the time of His arrest almost baffles comprehension. Almost, we say, for have we not learned from bitter experience the deceitfulness of our hearts, how feeble our faith is, how lamentably weak we are in the hour of trial and testing! But for the grace of God the truest trifle is sufficient to overturn us. Let the restraining and upholding power of God be withdrawn from us and how long would we stand?

The Lord Jesus had solemnly warned these disciples of their approaching cowardice "Then said Jesus unto them, All you shall be offended because of me this night: for it is written, I will smite the shepherd, and the sheep of the flock shall be scattered abroad" (Mat 26:31). And not Peter only but all of the apostles affirmed their determination to stand by Him "Peter said unto him, Though I should die with you, yet will I not deny you. Likewise, also said all the disciples" (Mat 26:35). Nevertheless, His word proved true, and they all basely deserted Him. And how this reflected upon His glory! By their sinful flight they exposed the Lord Jesus to the contempt and scoffs of His enemies. It was because of this we read, "The high priest then asked Jesus of his disciples" (John 18:19). It is not difficult to fill in the blanks. Doubtless Caiaphas inquired how many disciples He had, and what was become of them now? And what was the reason they had forsaken their Master, and left Him to shift for Himself when danger appeared? But observe that to this question the Savior made no reply. He would not accuse them to the common enemy though they had deserted Him!

They forsook Him because they were "offended" at Him "All you shall be offended because of me this night" (Mat 26:31): the Greek word here translated "offended" might well be rendered "scandalized." They were ashamed to be found in His company. They deemed it no longer safe to remain with Him. As He gave Himself up, they considered it advisable to provide as well as they might for themselves, and somewhere or other take refuge from the present storm which had overtaken Him. This from the human side.

From the divine side their forsaking of Christ was due to the suspension of God's preserving and upholding grace. They were not accustomed to forsaking Him. They never did so afterwards. They would not have done so now had there been influences of power, zeal, and love from Heaven upon them. But then how could Christ have borne the burden and heat of the day?

How should He have trod the winepress alone? How should His sorrows have been unmitigated if they had adhered faithfully to Him? No, no, it must not be. Christ must not have the least relief or comfort from any creature, and therefore that He might be left alone to grapple with the wrath of God and man, the Lord for a time withholds His strengthening influences from them; and then like Samson when he was shorn of his locks, they were as weak as other men. "Be strong in the Lord, and in the power of His might" says the apostle if that be withheld, our purposes and resolutions melt away before temptation, like snow before the sun.

Yet mark that the cowardice and infidelity of the apostles was only temporary. Later, they sought Him at the appointed place in Galilee (Mat 28:16). But is it not cheering to know that one of the Eleven did seek Him out before He rose in triumph from the tomb? Yes, sought Him while He yet hung on the Cross of shame! And who might it be supposed this one was? Which of the little band of apostles shall demonstrate the superiority of His love? Even if the sacred narrative had concealed his identity, it would not have been a difficult task to supply his name. The fact that the Scripture we are now considering shows us John at the foot of the Cross is one of the silent yet sufficient witnesses to the divine inspiration of the Bible. It is one of those undesigned harmonies of the Word which attests the super- human origin of the Scriptures. There is no hint that any other of the Eleven were around the Cross, but the thoughtful reader would expect to find there "the disciple whom Jesus loved." And there he was. John had returned to the Savior's side, and there receives from Him a blessed commission. How artless and how perfect are the silent harmonies of Scripture!

And now, once more, a brief word of exhortation. Is there one who reads these lines that has wandered away from the side of the Savior, who is no longer enjoying sweet communion with Him, who is, in a word, a backslider! Perhaps in the hour of trial you denied Him. Perhaps in the time of testing you failed. You have given more thought to your own interests than His. The honour of His name which you bear, has been lost sight of. O may the arrow of conviction now enter your conscience. May divine grace melt your heart. May the power of God draw you back to Christ, where alone your soul can find satisfaction and peace. Here is encouragement for you. Christ did not rebuke John on returning; instead, His wondrous grace bestowed on him an unspeakable privilege. Cease then your wanderings and return at once to Christ, and He will greet you with a word of welcome and cheer; and who knows but what He has some honorous commission awaiting you!

4. Here we discover an illustration of Christ's prudence. We have already seen how the act of Christ in committing Mary into the hands of His disciple was an expression of His tender love and foresight. For John to take charge of the widowed mother of the Savior was a blessed commission, and albeit, a precious legacy. When Christ said to him, "Behold your mother," it was as though He had said,

"Let her be to you as your own mother: Let your love for Me be now manifested in your tender regard for her." Yet there was far more behind this act of Christ than that.

Of old it had been predicted that the Lord Jesus should act wisely and discreetly. Through Isaiah God had said, "Behold, my servant shall deal prudently "(52:13). In commending His mother to the care

of His loved apostle, the Savior displayed wise discrimination in His choice of the one who was henceforth to be her guardian. Perhaps there was none who understood the Lord Jesus so well as His mother, and it is almost certain that none had apprehended His love so deeply as had John. We see therefore how they would be fit companions for each other, inasmuch as there was an intimate bond of common sympathy uniting them together and uniting them to Christ! Thus, there was none other so well suited to take care of Mary, none whose company she would find so congenial and on the other hand, there was none whose fellowship John would more enjoy.

Furthermore, it needs to be borne in mind that a wondrous and honorous work was waiting for John. Years later, the Lord Jesus was to reveal Himself to this apostle in glorious apocalypse. How better, then, could he equip himself for this than by being constantly with her who had lived in closest intimacy and fellowship with the Savior during the thirty years He had waited for the time to come when His work should begin! We can therefore see how that there was a significant appropriateness in bringing these two Mary and John together. Admire then the prudence of Christ's election of a home for Mary, and at the same time providing a companion for the disciple whom He loved, with whom he might have blessed spiritual fellowship.

Before passing to our next point, we may remark that this taking of Mary into his home throws light on an incident recorded in the next chapter of John's Gospel. In John 20 we learn of the visit of Peter and John to the empty sepulcher. John outran his companion and arrived first at the tomb, but went not in. Peter, characteristically, goes into the sepulcher, and notes the orderly arrangement of the clothes. Then enters John and he sees and "believed," for up to this time their faith had not grasped the promises of Christ's resurrection. Consequent on John's believing, we read, "Then the disciples went away again unto their own home" (John 20:10). We are not told why they did this, but in view of John 19:27 the explanation is obvious. There we are told that, "from that hour that disciple took her unto his own home," and now that he has learned the Savior is risen from the dead, he hastens back "home" to tell her the good news! Who more than she would rejoice at the glad tidings! This is another example of the silent and hidden harmonies of Scripture.

5. Here we see that spiritual relationships must not ignore the responsibilities of nature. The Lord Jesus was dying as the Savior for sinners. He was engaged in the most momentous and the most stupendous undertaking that this earth ever has or ever will witness. He was on the point of offering satisfaction to the outraged justice of God. He was just about to do that work for which the world had been made, for which the human race had been created, for which all the ages had waited, and for which He, the eternal Word, had become incarnate. Nevertheless, He does not overlook the responsibilities of natural ties; He fails not to make provision for her who, according to the flesh, was His mother.

There is a lesson here which many need to take to heart in these days. No duty, no work, however important it may be, can excuse us from discharging the obligations of nature, from caring for those who have fleshly claims upon us. They who go forth as missionaries to labour in heathen lands and who leave their children behind, or who send them back to the homeland to be cared for by strangers, are not following the steps of the Savior. Those women who spend most of their time at public meetings, even though they may be religious meetings, or who go down into the slums to minister to the poor and needy, to the neglect of their own family at home, do but bring reproach upon the name and cause of Christ. Those men, even though they stand at the forefront of Christian work, who are so busy preaching and teaching that they have no time to discharge the obligations that they owe to their own wives and children, need to study, and practice the principle exemplified here by Christ on the Cross.

6. Here we see a universal need exemplified. How different is the Mary of Scripture from the Mary of superstition! She was no proud Madonna but, like each of us, a member of a fallen race, a sinner both by nature and practice. Before the birth of Christ she declared, "My soul does magnify the Lord, and my spirit has rejoiced in God my Savior "(Luke 1:46-47). And now at the death of the Lord Jesus she is found before the Cross. The Word of God presents not the mother of Jesus as the Queen of angels decked with diadem, but as one who herself rejoiced in a Savior. It is true she is "blessed among (not "above") women," and that by virtue of the high honour of being the mother of the Redeemer; yet was she human, a real member of our fallen race, a sinner needing a Savior.

She stood by the Cross. And as she stood there the Savior exclaimed, "Woman, behold your son!" (John 19:26). There, summed up in a single word, is expressed the need of every descendant of Adam to turn the eye away from the world, off from self, and to look by faith to the Savior that died for sinners. There is the divine epitome of the way of salvation. Deliverance from the wrath to come, forgiveness of sins, acceptance with God, is obtained not by deed of merit, not by good works, not by religious ordinances; No, salvation comes by beholding "Behold the Lamb of God which takes away the sin of the world" (John 1:19). Just as the serpent-bitten Israelites in the wilderness were healed by a look, by a look at that which Jehovah had appointed to be the object of their faith, so today, redemption from the guilt and power of sin, emancipation from the curse of the broken Law and from the captivity of Satan, is to be found alone by faith in Christ, "As Moses lifted up the serpent in the wilderness, even so must the son of man be lifted up: that whoever believes in him should not perish, but have eternal life" (John 3:14-15). There is life in a look. Reader, have you thus beheld that divine sufferer? Have you seen Him dying on the Cross, the Just for the unjust, that He might bring us to God? Mary the mother of Christ needed to "behold" Him, and so do you. Then look, look unto Christ and be you saved!

7. Here we see the marvellous blending of Christ's perfections. This is one of the greatest wonders of His Person, the blending of the most perfect human affection with His divine glory. The very Gospel which most of all shows Him to be God, is here careful to prove He was man, the Word made flesh. Engaged as He was in a divine transaction, making atonement for all the sins of all His people, grappling with the powers of darkness yet amid it all, He has still the same human tenderness, which shows the perfection of the Man Jesus Christ.

The care for His mother in His dying hour was characteristic of all His conduct. Everything was natural and perfect. The unstudied simplicity about Him is most marked. There was nothing pompous or ostentatious. Many of His mightiest works were done on the highway, in the cottage, or among a little group of sufferers. Many of His words, which today are still unfathomable and exhaustless in their wealth of meaning, were uttered almost casually as He walked with a few friends. So, it was at the Cross. He was performing the mightiest work of all history; He was engaging in doing that, which in comparison, the creating of a world fade into utter insignificance, yet He forgets not to make provision for His mother much as He might have done had they been together in the home at Nazareth. Rightly was it said of old, "His name shall be called Wonderful "(Isa 9:6). Wonderful He was in all that He did. Wonderful He was in every relationship that He sustained. Wonderful He was in His person, and wonderful He was in His work. Wonderful was He in life, and wonderful was He in death. Let us wonder and adore.

4. The Word Of Anguish

"And about the ninth hour Jesus cried with a loud voice, Saying, Eli, Eli, lama sabachthani? that is to say, My God, my God, why has you forsaken me?" Matthew 27:46

"My God, my God, why have you forsaken me?" (Mat 27:46). These are words of startling import. The crucifixion of the Lord of Glory was the most extraordinary event that has ever happened on earth, and this cry of the suffering One was the most startling utterance of that appalling scene. That innocence should be condemned, that the guiltless should be persecuted, that a benefactor should be cruelly put to death, was no new event in history. From the murder of righteous Abel to that of Zechariah, there was a long list of such martyrdoms. But He who hung on this central Cross was no ordinary man, He was the Son of Man, the One in whom all excellencies met the Perfect One. Like His robe, His character was "without seam, woven from the top throughout" (John 19:23).

In the case of all other persecuted ones there were demerits and blemishes which might afford their murderers something to blame. But the judge of this One said, "I find no fault in him." And more: this sufferer was not only a perfect man, but He was the Son of God. Yet, it is not strange that man should wish to destroy God. "The fool has said in his heart, There is no God" (Psalm 14:1); such is his wish. But it is strange that He who was God manifest in the flesh should allow Himself to be so mistreated by His enemies. It is exceeding strange that the Father who delighted in Him, whose own voice had declared from the opened heavens, "This is my beloved Son, in whom I am well pleased," should deliver Him up to such a shameful death.

"My God, my God, why have you forsaken me? "These are the words of appalling woe. The very word "forsaken" is one of the most tragic in all human speech. The writer will not readily forget his sensation as he once passed through a town deserted of all its inhabitants, a forsaken city. What calamities are conjured up by this word, a man forsaken of his friends, a wife forsaken by her husband, a child forsaken by its parents! But a creature forsaken by its Creator, a man forsaken of God O this is the most frightful of all. This is the evil of all evils. This is the climactic calamity. True, fallen man, in his unrenewed condition, does not so deem it. But he, who in some measure at least, has learned that God is the sum of all perfections, the fount and goal of all excellencies, he whose cry is "As the heart pants after the water brooks, so pants my soul after you, O God" (Psalm 42:1), is ready to endorse what has just been said. The cry of saints in all ages has been, "Forsake us not, O God." For the Lord to hide His face from us but for a moment is unbearable. If this is true of renewed sinners, how infinitely more so of the beloved Son of the Father!

He who hung there on the accursed tree had been from all eternity the object of the Father's love. To employ the language of Proverbs 8, the suffering Savior was the one who "was by him, as one brought up with him," He was "daily his delight." His own joy had been to behold the Father's countenance. The Father's presence had been His home, the Father's bosom His dwelling-place; the Father's glory He had shared before ever the world was. During the thirty and three years the Son had been on earth, He enjoyed unbroken communion with the Father. Never a thought that was out of harmony with the Father's mind, never a volition but what originated in the Father's will, never a moment spent out of His conscious presence. What then must it have meant to be forsaken now by God! Ah, the hiding of God's face from Him was the most bitter ingredient of that cup which the Father had given the Redeemer to drink.

"My God, my God, why have you forsaken me? "These are words of unequalled pathos. They mark the climax of His sufferings. The soldiers had cruelly mocked Him: they had arrayed Him with the crown of thorns, they had scourged and buffeted Him, they even went so far as to spit upon Him and pluck off His hair. They despoiled Him of His garments and put Him to open shame. Yet He suffered it all in silence. They pierced His hands and feet, yet did He endure the Cross, despising the shame. The vulgar crowd taunted Him, and the thieves which were crucified with Him flung the same taunts into His face; yet He opened not His mouth. In response to all that He suffered at the hands of men, not a cry escaped His lips. But now, as the concentrated wrath of Heaven descends upon Him, He cries, "My God, my God, why have you forsaken me?" Surely this is a cry that ought to melt the hardest heart!

"My God, my God, why have you forsaken me? "These are the words of deepest mystery. Of old the Lord Jehovah forsook not His people. Again and again, he was their refuge in trouble. When Israel was in cruel bondage they cried unto God, and He heard them. When they stood helpless before the Red Sea, He came to their aid and delivered them from their enemies. When the three Hebrews were cast into the fiery furnace, the Lord was with them. But here, at the Cross, there ascends a more plaintive and agonizing cry than ever went up from the land of Egypt, yet there was no response! Here was a situation far more alarming than the Red Sea crisis: enemies more relentless beset this One, yet there was no deliverance! Here was a fire that burned infinitely fiercer than Nebuchadnezzar's furnace, but there was no one by His side to comfort! He is abandoned by God!

Yes, this cry of the suffering Savior is deeply mysterious. At first, He had cried, "Father, forgive them, for they know not what they do," and this we can understand, for it well accords with His compassionate heart. Again, He had opened His mouth, to say to the repentant thief, "Truly I say unto you, Today shall you be with me in paradise," and this too, we can well understand, for it was in full keeping with His grace toward sinners. Once more His lips moved to His mother, "Woman, behold your son;" to the beloved John, "Behold your mother" and this also we can appreciate. But the next time He opens His mouth a cry is made which startles and staggers us. Of old David said, "I have never seen the righteous forsaken," but here we behold the Righteous One, forsaken!

"My God, my God, why have you forsaken me? "These are words of profoundest solemnity. This was a cry which made the very earth tremble, and that reverberated throughout the entire universe. Ah, what mind is sufficient for contemplating this wonder of wonders! What mind is capable of analysing the meaning of this amazing cry which rent the awful darkness! "Why have you forsaken me?" are words which conduct us into the Holy of Holies. Here, if anywhere, it is supremely fitting that we remove the shoes of carnal inquisitiveness. Speculation is profane; we can but wonder and worship.

But though these words are of startling import, appalling woe, deepest mystery, unique pathos, and profound solemnity, yet are we not left in ignorance as to their meaning. True, this cry was deeply mysterious, yet is it capable of most blessed solution. The Holy Scriptures leave it impossible to doubt that these words of unequalled grief were both the fullest manifestation of divine love and the most awe-inspiring display of God's inflexible justice. May every thought be now brought into captivity to Christ, and may our hearts be duly solemnized as we take a closer view of this fourth utterance of the dying Savior.

"My God, my God, why have you forsaken me?"

1. Here we see the awfulness of sin and the character of its wages. The Lord Jesus was crucified at mid-day, and in the light of Calvary everything was revealed in its true character. There the very nature of things was fully and finally exhibited. The depravity of the human heart, its hatred of God, its base ingratitude, its loving of darkness rather than light, its preference of a murderer for the Prince of life was fearfully displayed. The awful character of the devil, his hostility

against God, his insatiable enmity against Christ, his power to put it into the heart of man to betray the Savior was completely exposed. So, too, the perfections of the divine nature. God's ineffable holiness, His inflexible justice, His terrible wrath, His matchless grace was fully made known. And there it was also, that sin its baseness, its turpitude, its lawlessness was plainly exhibited. Here we are shown the fearful lengths to which sin will go. In its first manifestation it took the form of suicide, for Adam destroyed his own spiritual life; next we see it in the form of fratricide. Cain slaying his own brother; but at the Cross the climax is reached in deicide man crucifying the Son of God.

But not only do we see the heinousness of sin at the Cross, but there we also discover the character of its awful wages. "The wage of sin is death" (Rom 6:23). Death is the entail of sin. "By one man sin entered into the world, and death by sin and so, death passed upon all men, for that all have sinned" (Rom 5:12). Had there been no sin there would have been no death.

But what is death? Is it that dreadful silence which reigns supreme after the last breath is drawn and the body lies motionless? Is it that ghastly pallor which comes over the face as the blood ceases to circulate and the eyes remain expressionless? Yes, it is that, but much more. Something far more pathetic and tragic than physical dissolution is contained in the term.

The wage of sin is spiritual death. Sin separates from God, Who is the fount of all life. This was shown forth in Eden. Previous to the Fall, Adam enjoyed blessed fellowship with his Maker, but in the early eve of that day that marked the entrance of sin into our world, as the Lord God entered the Garden and His voice was heard by our first parents, the guilty pair hid themselves among the trees of the garden. No longer might they enjoy communion with Him Who is always light, instead, they are alienated from Him. So, too, was it with Cain: when interrogated by the Lord he said, "From your face shall I be hid" (Gen 4:14) Sin excludes from God's presence. That was the great lesson taught Israel. Jehovah's throne was in their midst, yet it was not accessible. He abode between the cherubim in the Holy of Holies and into it none might come, saving the high priest, and he but one day in the year bearing blood with him. The veil which hung both in the tabernacle and in the temple, barring access to the throne of God, witnessed to the solemn fact that sin separates from Him.

The wage of sin is death, not only physical but spiritual death, not merely natural but essentially penal death. What is physical death? It is the separation of the soul and spirit from the body. So penal death is the separation of the soul and spirit from God. The Word of Truth speaks of her that lives in pleasure as being "dead while she lives" (1 Timothy 5:6). Note, too, how that wonderful parable of the prodigal son illustrates the force of the term "death." After the return of the prodigal the father said, "This my son was dead, and is alive again; he was lost, and is found" (Luke 15:24). While he was in the "far country" he had not ceased to exist; no, he was not dead physically, but spiritually he was alienated and separated from his father!

Now on the Cross the Lord Jesus was receiving the wages which were due His people. He had no sin of His own, for He was the Holy One of God. But he was bearing our sins in His own body on the tree (1 Peter 2:24). He had taken our place and was suffering, the Just for the unjust. He was bearing the chastisement of our peace and the wages of our sins, the suffering and chastisement which were due us, was "death." Not merely physical but penal; and, as we have said, this meant separation from God, and hence it was that the Savior cried, "My God, my God, why have you forsaken me?"

So, too, will it be with the finally impenitent. The awful doom awaiting the lost is thus set forth, "who shall be punished with everlasting destruction from the presence of the Lord, and from the glory of his power" (2 Thessalonians 1:9) eternal separation from Him Who is the fount of all goodness and the source of all blessing. Unto the wicked Christ shall say, "Depart from me, you cursed" banishment from His presence, an eternal exile from God, is what awaits the damned. This is the reason why the Lake of Fire, the eternal abode of those whose names are not written in the Book of Life is designated "the second death" (Rev 20:14). Not that there will be an extinction of being, but everlasting separation from the Lord of life, a separation which Christ suffered for three hours as He hung in the sinner's place. At the Cross, then, Christ received the wages of sin.

"My God, my God, why have you forsaken me?"

2. Here we see the absolute holiness and inflexible justice of God. The tragedy of Calvary must be viewed from at least four different viewpoints. At the Cross man did a work: he displayed his depravity by taking the perfect One and with "wicked hands" nailing Him to the tree. At the Cross Satan did a work: he manifested his insatiable enmity against the woman's seed by bruising His heel. At the Cross the Lord Jesus did a work: He died, the Just for the unjust that He might bring us to God. At the Cross God did a work: He exhibited His holiness and satisfied His justice by pouring out His wrath on the One who was made sin for us.

What human pen is able or fit to write about the unsullied holiness of God! So holy is God that mortal man cannot look upon Him in His essential Being and live. So holy is God that the very heavens are not clean in His sight. So holy is God that even the seraphim veil their faces before Him. So holy is God that when Abraham stood before Him, he cried, "I am but dust and ashes" (Gen 18:27). So holy is God that when Job came into His presence he said, "Wherefore I abhor myself" (Job 42:6). So holy is God that when Isaiah had a vision of His glory he exclaimed, "Woe is me! for I am undone...for mine eyes have seen the King, the Lord of hosts" (Isa 6:5). So holy is God that when Daniel beheld Him in theophanic manifestations he declared, "there remained no strength in me: for my loveliness was turned in me into corruption" (Dan 10:8). So holy is God that we are told, "He is of purer eyes than to behold evil and cannot look on iniquity " (Hab 1:13). And it was because the Savior was bearing our sins that the thrice holy God would not look on Him, turned His face from Him, forsook Him. The Lord made to meet on Christ the iniquities of us all: and our sins being on Him as our substitute, the divine wrath against our offences must be spent upon our sin-offering.

"My God, my God, why have you forsaken me?" That was a question which none of those around the Cross could have answered; it was a question which, at that time, none of the apostles could have answered; yes, it was a question which had puzzled the angels in Heaven to make reply to. But the Lord Jesus had answered His own question, and His answer is found in Psalm Twenty-two. This Psalm furnished a most wonderful prophetic fore view of His sufferings. The Psalm opens with the very words of our Savior's fourth Cross-utterance, and it is followed by further agonizing sobs in the same strain until: at verse three we find Him saying, "But you are holy." He complains not of injustice; instead, He acknowledges God's righteousness You are holy and just in exacting all the debt at My hand which I am Surety for; I have all the sins of all My people to answer for, and therefore I justify You, O God, in giving Me this stroke from Your awakened sword. You are Holy; You are clear when You judge.

At the Cross, then, as nowhere else, we see the infinite malignity of sin and the justice of God in the punishment thereof. Was the old world over-flown with water? were Sodom and Gomorrah destroyed by a storm of fire and brimstone? were the plagues sent upon Egypt? and were Pharaoh and his hosts drowned in the Red Sea? In these may the demerit of sin and God's hatred thereof be seen; but much more so here is Christ forsaken of God. Go to Golgotha and see the man that is Jehovah's fellow drinking up the cup of His Father's indignation, smitten by the sword of divine justice, bruised by the Lord Himself, suffering unto death, for God "spared not his own Son" when He hung in the sinner's place.

Behold how nature herself had anticipated the dreadful tragedy the very contour of the ground is like unto a skull. Behold the earth trembling beneath the mighty load of outpoured wrath. Behold the heavens as the sun turns away from such a scene, and the land is covered with darkness. Here may we see the dreadful anger of a sin-avenging God. Not all the thunderbolts of divine judgment which were let loose in Old Testament times, not all the vials of wrath which shall yet be poured forth on an apostate Christendom during the unparalleled horrors of the Great Tribulation, not all the weeping and wailing and gnashing of teeth of the damned in the Lake of Fire ever gave, or ever will give such a demonstration of God's inflexible justice and ineffable holiness, of His infinite hatred of sin, as did the wrath of God which flamed against His own Son on the Cross. Because He was enduring sin's terrific judgment, He was forsaken of God. He who was the Holy One, whose own abhorrence of sin was infinite, who was purity incarnate (1 John 3:3) was "made sin for us" (2 Corinthians 5:21). Therefore, did He bow before the storm of wrath, in which was displayed the divine displeasure against the countless sins of a great multitude whom no man can number. This, then, is the true explanation of Calvary. God's holy character could not do less than judge sin, even though it be found on Christ Himself. At the Cross, then, God's justice was satisfied, and His holiness vindicated.

"My God, my God, why have you forsaken me?"

3. Here we see the explanation of Gethsemane. As our blessed Lord approached the Cross, the horizon darkened for Him more and more. From earliest infancy He had suffered from man; from the beginning of His public ministry, He had suffered from Satan; but at the Cross He was to suffer at the hand of God. Jehovah Himself was to bruise the Savior, and it was this which overshadowed everything else. In Gethsemane He entered the gloom of the three hours of darkness on the Cross. That is why He left the three disciples on the outskirts of the garden, for He must tread the winepress alone. "My soul is exceeding sorrowful," He cried. This was no shrinking horror in anticipation of a cruel death. It was not the thought of betrayal by His own familiar friend, nor of the desertion by His cherished disciples in the hour of crisis, nor was it the expectation of the mocking's and

reviling's, the stripes, and the nails, that overwhelmed His soul. No, all of this keenest anguish as it must have been to His sensitive spirit, was as nothing compared with what He had to endure as the Sin-bearer.

"Then comes Jesus with them unto a place called Gethsemane, and says unto the disciples, Sit you here, while I go and pray yonder. And he took with him, Peter, and the two sons of Zebedee, and began to be sorrowful and very heavy. Then says he unto them, my soul is exceeding sorrowful, even unto death: tarry you here, and watch with me. And he went a little farther, and fell on his face, and prayed, saying, O my Father, if it be possible, let this cup pass from me: nevertheless, not as I will, but as you will" (Mat 26:36-39). Here He views the black clouds arising, He sees the dreadful storm coming. He premeditated the inexpressible horror of that three hours of darkness and all they held. "My soul is exceeding sorrowful," He cries. The Greek is most emphatic. He was begirt with sorrow. He was plunged over head and ears in the anticipated wrath of God. All the faculties and powers of His soul were wrung with anguish. St. Mark employs another form of expression "He began to be sore amazed" (14:33). The original signifies the greatest extremity of amazement, such as makes one's hair stand on end and their flesh to creep. And, Mark adds, "and to be very heavy," which denotes there was an utter sinking of spirit; His heart was melted like wax at sight of the terrible cup.

But the evangelist Luke uses the strongest terms of all: "And being in an agony he prayed more earnestly: and his sweat was as it were great drops of blood falling down to the ground" (Luke 22:44). The Greek word for "agony" here, means to be engaged in a combat. Before, He had combated the oppositions of men and the oppositions of the devil, but now He faces the cup which God gives Him to drink. It was the cup which contained the undiluted wrath of a sin-hating God. This explains why He said, "If it be possible let this cup pass from me." The "cup" is the symbol of Communion, and there could be no communion in His wrath, but only in His love.

Notwithstanding, though it means being cut off from communion He adds, "Nevertheless not as I will, but as you will."

Yet so great was His agony that "His sweat was as it were great drops of blood falling down to the ground." We think that there can be little doubt that the Savior shed actual drops of blood. There would be little meaning in saying that His sweat resembled blood but was not really that. It seems to us the emphasis is on the word "blood." He shed blood just like great beads of water in ordinary cases. And here we see the fitness of the place chosen to be the scene of this terrible but preliminary suffering. "Gethsemane" ah, your name betrays you! It means the olive-press. It was the place where the lifeblood of the olives was pressed out drop by drop! The chosen place was well named then. It was indeed a fit footstool to the Cross, a footstool of agony unutterable and unparalleled. On the Cross then, Christ drained the cup which was presented to Him in Gethsemane.

"My God, my God, why have you forsaken me?"

4. Here we see the Savior's unswerving fidelity to God. The forsaking of the Redeemer by God was a solemn fact, and an experience which left Him nothing but the supports of His faith. Our Savior's position on the Cross was absolutely unique. This may readily be seen by contrasting His own words spoken during His public ministry with those uttered on the Cross itself. Formerly He said, "And I know that you hear me always" (John 11:42); now He cries, "O my God, I cry in the daytime, but you hear not "(Psalm 22:2)! Formerly He said, "And he who sent me is with me: the father has not left me alone" (John 8:29); now He cries, "My God, my God, why have you forsaken me?" He had absolutely nothing now to rest upon save His Father's covenant and promise; and in His cry of anguish His faith is made manifest. It was a cry of distress but not of distrust. God had withdrawn from Him, but mark how His soul still cleaves to God. His faith triumphed by laying hold of God even amid the darkness. "My God," He says, "My God," You with Whom is infinite and everlasting strength; You who have hitherto supported My manhood, and

according to Your promise upheld Your servant O be not far from Me now. My God, I lean on You. When all visible and sensible comforts had disappeared, to the invisible support and refuge of His faith did the Savior betake Himself.

In the Twenty-second Psalm the Savior's unswerving fidelity to God is most apparent. In this precious Psalm the depths of His heart are told out. Hear Him: "Our fathers trusted in you: they trusted, and you did deliver them. They cried unto you and were delivered: they trusted in you and were not confounded. But I am a worm, and no man; a reproach of men, and despised of the people. All they that see me laugh me to scorn: they shoot out the lip, they shake the head, saying, He trusted on the Lord that he would deliver him: let him deliver him, seeing he delighted in him. But you are he who took me out of the womb: You did make me hope when I was upon my mother's breasts. I was cast upon you from the womb: You are my God from my mother's belly" (Psalm 22:4-10). The very point His enemies sought to make against Him was His faith in God. They taunted Him with His "trust" in Jehovah if He really trusted in the Lord, the Lord would deliver Him. But the Savior continued trusting though there was no deliverance, trusted though "forsaken" for a season! He had been cast upon God from the womb and He is still found cast upon God in the hour of His death.

He continues, "Be not far from me; for trouble is near; for there is none to help. Many bulls have compassed me: strong bulls of Bashan have beset me round. They gaped upon me with their mouths, as a ravening and a roaring lion. I am poured out like water and all my bones are out of joint; my heart is like wax; it is melted in the midst of my affections. My strength is dried up like a potsherd; and my tongue cleaves to my jaws; and you has brought me into the dust of death. For dogs have compassed me: the assembly of the wicked have enclosed me: they pierced my hands and my feet. I may tell all my bones: they look and stare upon me. They part my garments among them and cast lots upon my vesture. But be not you far from me, O Lord; O my strength, haste you to help me. Deliver my soul from the sword; My darling from the power of the dog" (Psalm 22:11-20). Job had said of God, "Though he slay me yet will I trust him," and though the wrath of God against sin rested upon Christ, still He trusted. Yes, His faith did more than trust, it triumphed "Save me from the lion's mouth: for you have heard me from the horns of the unicorns" (Psalm 22:21).

O what an example has the Savior left His people! It is comparatively easy to trust God while the sun is shining, the test comes when all is dark. But a faith that does not rest on God in adversity as well as in prosperity is not the faith of God's elect: We must have faith to live by true faith if we would have faith to die by. The Savior had been cast upon God from His mother's womb, had been cast upon God moment by moment all through those thirty-three years; what wonder then that the hour of death finds Him still cast upon God. Fellow-Christian, all may be dark with you, you may no longer behold the light of God's countenance. Providence seems to frown upon you, notwithstanding, say still Eli, Eli, my God, my God.

"My God, my God, why have you forsaken me?"

5. Here we may see the basis of our salvation. God is Holy and therefore He will not look upon sin. God is Just and therefore He judges sin wherever it is found. But God is Love as well: God delights in mercy, and therefore infinite wisdom devised a way whereby justice might be satisfied, and mercy left free to flow out to guilty sinners. This way was the way of substitution, the Just suffering for the unjust. The Son of God Himself was the one selected to be the substitute, for none other would suffice. Through Nahum, the question had been asked, "Who can stand before his indignation? and who can abide in the fierceness of his anger?" (1:6). This question received its answer in the person of our Lord and Savior Jesus Christ. He alone could "stand." One only could bear the curse and yet rise a victor above it. One only could endure all the avenging wrath and yet magnify the Law and make it honourable. One only could suffer his heel to be bruised by Satan and yet in that bruising destroy him that

had the power of death. God laid help upon One that was "mighty" (Psalm 89:19), One who was no less than the Fellow of Jehovah, the Radiance of His glory, the exact Impress of His Person. Thus, we see that boundless love, inflexible justice and omnipotent power all combined to make possible the salvation of those who believe.

At the Cross all our iniquities were laid upon Christ, and therefore did divine judgment fall upon Him. There was no way of transferring sin without also transferring its penalty. Both sin and its punishment were transferred to the Lord Jesus. On the Cross, Christ was making atoning sacrifice, and atoning sacrifice is solely Godwards. It was a question of meeting the claims of God's holiness; it was a matter of satisfying the demands of His justice. Not only was Christ's blood shed for us, but it was also shed for God: He "has given himself for us an offering and sacrifice to God for a sweet-smelling savor" (Eph 5:2). Thus, it was foreshadowed on the memorable night of the Passover in Egypt: the lamb's blood must be where God's eye could see it "When I see the blood, I will pass over you!"

The death of Christ on the Cross was a death of the curse: "Christ has redeemed us from the curse of the Law, being made a curse for us for it is written, Cursed is every one that hangs on a tree" (Gal 3:13). The "curse" is alienation from God. This is apparent from the words which Christ will yet speak to those that shall stand on His left hand in the day of His power "Depart from me, you cursed" He will say (Mat 25:41). The curse is exile from the presence and glory of God. This explains the meaning of a number of Old Testament types. The bullock, which was slain on the annual Day of Atonement, after its blood had been sprinkled upon and before the mercy-seat, was removed to a place without [outside] the camp" (Lev 16:27), and there its entire carcass was burned. It was in the centre of the camp that God had His dwelling-place, and exclusion from the camp was banishment from the presence of God. Thus, it was, too, with the leper. "All the days wherein the plague shall be in him he shall be defiled; he is unclean: he shall dwell alone; without the camp shall his habitation be" (Lev 13:46) this because the leper was the embodied type of the sinner.

Here also is the anti-type of the "brazen serpent" (Num 21:8-9). Why did God instruct Moses to set a "serpent" on a pole, and bid the bitten Israelites look upon it? Imagine a serpent as a type of Christ, the Holy One of God! Yes, but it represented Him as "made a curse for us," for the serpent was the reminder of the curse. On the Cross, then, Christ was fulfilling these Old Testament foreshadowing's. He was "outside the camp" (compare Hebrews 13:12) separated from the presence of God. He was as the "leper" made sin for us. He was as the "brazen serpent" made a curse for us. Hence too, the deep meaning of the crown of thorns, the symbol of the curse! Lifted up, His brow encircled with thorns, to show He was bearing the curse for us.

Here, too, is the significance of the three hours darkness which lay over the land as a pall of death. It was supernatural darkness. It was not night, for the sun was at its zenith. As Mr. Spurgeon well said, "It was midnight at midday." It was no eclipse. Competent astronomers tell us that at the time of the crucifixion the moon was at her farthest from the sun. But this cry of Christ's gives the meaning of the darkness, as the darkness gives us the meaning of that bitter cry. One thing alone can explain this darkness, as one thing alone can interpret this cry that Christ had taken the place of guilty and lost ones, that He was in the place of sin-bearing, that He was enduring the judgment due His people, that He Who knew no sin was "made sin" for us.

That cry was uttered that we might be allowed to know of what passed there. It was the manifestation of atonement, so to speak, for three (three hours) is ever the number of manifestations. God is light and the "darkness" is the natural sign of His turning away (1 John 1:5). The Redeemer was left alone with the sinner's sin; that was the explanation of the three hours' darkness. Just as there will rest upon the damned a twofold misery in the Lake of Fire, namely, the pain of sense and the pain of loss so, upon Christ answerably, He suffered the outpoured wrath of God and also the withdrawal of His presence and fellowship.

For the believer, the Cross is interpreted in Galatians 2:20 "I am crucified with Christ." He was my substitute; God reckoned me one with the Savior. His death was mine. He was wounded for my transgressions and bruised for my iniquities. Sin was not pushed away but put away. As another has said, "Because God judged sin on the Son, He now accepts the believing sinner in the Son." Our life is hid with Christ in God (Col 3:3). I am shut up in Christ because Christ was shut out from God.

"He suffered in our stead, He saved His people; thus, The curse that fell upon His head, was due by right to us. The storm that bowed His blessed head, is hushed forever now And rest divine is mine instead, while glory crowns His brow."

Here then is the basis of our salvation. Our sins have been borne. God's claims against us have been fully met. Christ was forsaken of God for a season that we might enjoy His presence forever. "My God, my God, why have you forsaken me?" Let every believing soul make answer: He entered the awful Darkness that I might walk in the Light; He drank the cup of woe that I might drink the cup of joy; He was forsaken that I might be forgiven!

"My God, my God, why have you forsaken me?"

6. Here we see the supreme evidence of Christ's love for us. "Greater love has no man than this, that a man lay down his life for his friends" (John 15:13). But the greatness of Christ's love can be estimated only when we are able to measure what was involved in the "laying down" of His love. As we have seen, it meant much more than physical death, even though that be of unspeakable shame and indescribable suffering. It meant that He took our place and was "made sin" for us, and what this involved can be judged only in the light of His person. Picture a perfectly honourable and virtuous woman compelled to endure for a season association with the most vile and impure. Imagine her shut up in a den of iniquity, surrounded

by the course of all men and women, and with no way of escape. Can you estimate her abhorrence of the foul-mouthed oaths, the drunken revelry, the obscene surroundings? Can you form an opinion of what a pure woman would suffer in her soul amid such impurity? But the illustration falls far short, for there is no woman absolutely pure honourable, virtuous, morally pure, yes; but pure in the sense of being sinless, spiritually pure, no. But Christ was pure; absolutely pure. He was the Holy One. He had an infinite abhorrence of sin. He loathed it. His holy soul shrank from it. But on the Cross our iniquities were all laid upon Him, and sin that vile thing enrapt itself around Him like a horrible serpent's coils. And yet, He willingly suffered for us! Why? Because He loved us: "Having loved his own which were in the world, he loved them unto the end" (John 13:1).

But more: the greatness of Christ's love for us can be estimated only when we are able to measure the wrath of God that was poured upon Him. This it was from which His soul shrank. What this meant to Him, what it cost Him, may be learned in part by a perusal of the Psalms in which we are permitted to hear some of His pathos-filled soliloquies and petitions to God.

Speaking anticipatively, the Lord Jesus Himself by the Spirit cried through David, "Save me, O, God; for the waters are come in unto my soul. I sink in deep mire, where there is no standing: I am come into deep waters, where the floods overflow me. I am weary of my crying: My throat is dried: Mine eyes fail while I wait for my God...Deliver me out of the mire and let me not sink let me be delivered from them that hate me, and out of the deep waters. Let not the water-flood overflow me, neither let the deep swallow me up, and let not the pit shut her mouth upon me...Hide not your face from your servant; for I am in trouble; hear me speedily. Draw near unto my soul and redeem it: deliver me because of my enemies. You have known my reproach, and my shame, and my dishonour: Mine adversaries are all before you. Reproach has broken my heart; and I am full of heaviness: and I looked for some to take pity, but there was none; and for comforters, but I found none" (Psalm 69:1-3, 14-15, 17-20). And again, "Deep calls unto deep at the noise of your waterspouts; All your waves and your billows are gone over me" (Psalm 42:7).

God's abhorrence of sin swept forth and broke like a descending deluge upon the Sin-bearer. Looking forward to the awful anguish of the Cross, He cried through Jeremiah, "Is it nothing to you, all you that pass by? behold, and see if there be any sorrow like unto my sorrow, which is done unto me, with which the Lord has afflicted me in the day of his fierce anger "(Lam 1:12). These are a few of the intimations we have by which we can judge of the unspeakable horror with which the Holy One contemplated those three hours on the Cross, hours into which was condensed the equivalent of an eternal Hell. The Beloved of the Father must have the light of God's countenance hidden from Him; He must be left alone in the outer darkness.

Here was love matchless and unmeasured. "If it be possible let this cup pass from me," He cried. But it was not possible that His people should be saved unless He drained that awful cup of woe and wrath. And because there was none other who could drink it, He drained it. Blessed be His name! Where sin had brought men, Love brought the Savior.

"My God, my God, why have you forsaken me?"

7. Here we see the destruction of the "larger hope." This cry of the Savior foretells the final condition of every lost soul forsaken of God! Faithfulness compels us to warn the reader against the false teaching of the day. We are told that God loves everybody, and that He is too merciful to ever carry out the threatening's of His Word. This is precisely how the old Serpent argued with Eve. God had said, "In the day you eat thereof you shall surely die." The serpent said, "You shall not surely die." But whose word proved true? Not the devils, for he is a liar from the beginning. God's threat was fulfilled, and our first parents died spiritually in the day that they disobeyed His command. Thus, will it prove in a coming day. God is merciful: the fact that He

has provided a Savior, reader, proves it. The fact that He invites you to receive Christ as your Savior evidence His mercy. The fact that He has been so longsuffering with you, has borne with your stubborn rebellion until now, has prolonged your day of grace to this moment, proves it. But there is a limit to God's mercy. The day of mercy will soon be ended. The door of hope will soon be closed fast. Death may speedily cut you off, and after death is "the judgment." And in the Day of Judgment, God will deal in justice and not in mercy. He will avenge the mercy you have scorned. He will execute the sentence of condemnation already passed upon you: "He who believes not shall be damned" (Mar 16:16; John 3:18).

We will not repeat again what has already been said at length, sufficient now to remind the reader once more, how this cry of Christ's witnesses to God's hatred of sin. Because He is holy and just, God must judge sin wherever it is found. If then God spared not the Lord Jesus when sin was found on Him, what possible hope is there, unsaved reader, that He will spare you when you stand before Him at the Great White Throne with sin upon you? If God poured out His wrath on Christ while He hung as surety for His people, be assured that He will most certainly pour out His wrath on you if you die in your sins. The Word of Truth is explicit "He who believes not the Son shall not see life; but the wrath of God abides on him" (John 3:36). God "spared not "His own Son when He took the sinner's place, nor will He spare him who rejects the Savior. Christ was separated from God for three hours, and if you finally reject Him as your Savior, you will be separated from God forever "Who shall be punished with everlasting destruction from the presence of the Lord" (2 Thessalonians 1:9).

"My God, my God, why have you forsaken me?"

Here was a cry of desolation Reader, may you never echo it. Here was a cry of separation Reader, may you never experience it. Here was a cry of expiation Reader, may you appropriate its saving virtues!

✦✦✦

5. The Word Of Suffering

"Jesus knowing that all things were now accomplished, that the scripture might be fulfilled, says, I thirst." John 19:28

"I thirst." These words were spoken by the suffering Savior a little before He bowed the head and gave up the spirit. They are recorded only by the evangelist John and, as we shall see, it is fitting they should have a place in his Gospel, for they not only evidence His humanity but bring out His divine glory too.

"I thirst." What a text for a sermon! A short one it is true, yet how comprehensive, how expressive, and how tragic! The Maker of Heaven and earth with parched lips! The Lord of Glory in need of a drink! The Beloved of the Father crying "I thirst!" What a scene! What a word is this! Plainly, no uninspired pen drew such a picture.

Of old the Spirit of God moved David to say of the coming Messiah, "They gave me also gall for my meat; and in my thirst they gave me vinegar to drink" (Psalm 69:21). How marvellously complete was the prophetic fore view! No essential item was missing from it. Every important detail of the great Tragedy had been written down beforehand. The betrayal by a familiar friend (Psalm 41:9), the forsaking of the disciples through being offended at Him (Psalm 31:11), the false accusations (Psalm 35:11), the silence before His judges (Isa 53:7), the being proven guiltless (Isa 53:9), the numbering of Him with transgressors (Isa 53:12), the being crucified (Psalm

22:16), the mockery of the spectators (Psalm 109:25), the taunt of non-deliverance (Psalm 22:7-8), the gambling for His garments (Psalm 22:18), the prayer for His enemies (Isa 53:12), the being forsaken of God (Psalm 22:1), the thirsting (Psalm 69:21), the yielding of His spirit into the hands of the Father (Psalm 31:5), the bones not broken (Psalm 34:20), the burial in a rich man's tomb (Isa 53:9) all plainly foretold centuries before they came to pass. What convincing evidence of the divine inspiration of the Scriptures! "How firm a foundation, you saints of the Lord, is laid for your faith in His excellent Word!"

"I thirst." The fact that this is recorded as one of the seven cross-utterances of our Lord intimates that it is a word of precious meaning, a word to be treasured up in our hearts, a word deserving of prolonged meditation. We have seen that each of the previous sayings of the suffering Savior has much to teach us; surely this one can be no exception. What then are we to gather from it? What are the lessons which this fifth Crossword teaches us? May the Spirit of Truth illumine our understanding as we endeavour to fix our attention upon it.

"I thirst."

1. Here we have an evidence of Christ's humanity. The Lord Jesus was very God of very God, but He was also very man of very man. This is something to be believed and not for proud reason to speculate upon. The person of our adorable Savior is not a fit object for intellectual diagnosis; rather must we bow before Him in worship. He Himself warned us, "No man knows the son, but the Father" (Mat 11:27). And again, the Spirit of God through the apostle Paul declares, "Without controversy great is the mystery of godliness: God was manifest in the flesh" (1 Timothy 3:16). While then there is much about the person of Christ which we cannot fathom with our own understanding, yet there is everything about Him to admire and adore: foremost are His deity and humanity, and the perfect union of these two in one person. The Lord Jesus was not a divine man, nor a humanized God;

He was the Godman. Forever God, and now forever man. When the Beloved of the Father became incarnate, He did not cease to be God, nor did He lay aside any of His divine attributes, though He did strip Himself of the glory which He had with the Father before the world was. But in the incarnation, the Word became flesh and tabernacled among men. He ceased not to be all that He was previously, but He took to Himself that which He had not before perfect humanity.

The deity and humanity of the Savior were each contemplated in Messianic prediction. Prophecy represented the coming One sometimes as divine, sometimes as human. He was the Branch "of the Lord" (Isa 4:2). He was the Wonderful Counsellor, the Mighty God, the Father of the ages (Hebrews), the "Prince of Peace" (Isa 9:6). The One who was to come forth out of Bethlehem and be Ruler in Israel, was One whose goings forth had been from the days of eternity (Mic 5:2). It was none less than Jehovah Himself who was to come suddenly to the temple (Mal 3:1). Yet, on the other hand, He was the woman's "seed" (Gen 3:15); a prophet like unto Moses (Deu 18:18); a lineal descendant of David (2 Samuel 7:12-13). He was Jehovah's "servant" (Isa 42:1). He was "the man of sorrows" (Isa 53:3). And it is in the New Testament we see these two different sets of prophecy harmonized.

The one born at Bethlehem was the divine Word. The incarnation does not mean that God manifested Himself as a man. The Word became flesh; He became what He was not before, though He never ceased to be all He was previously. He who was in the form of God and thought it not robbery to be equal with God, "made himself of no reputation, and took upon him the form of a servant, and was made in the likeness of men" (Phi 2:6-7). The Babe of Bethlehem was Immanuel God with us. He was more than a manifestation of God He was God manifest in the flesh. He was both Son of God and Son of Man. Not two separate personalities, but one Person possessing two natures the divine and the human.

While here on earth, the Lord Jesus gave full proof of His deity. He spoke with divine wisdom; He acted in divine holiness; He exhibited divine power; and He displayed divine love. He read men's minds, moved men's hearts, and compelled men's wills. When He was pleased to exert His power, all nature was subject to His bidding. A word from Him and disease fled, a storm was stilled, the devil left Him, the dead were raised to life. So truly was He God manifest in the flesh, He could say, "he who has seen me, has seen the Father."

So, too, while He tabernacled among men, the Lord Jesus gave full proof of His humanity sinless humanity. He entered this world as a babe and was "wrapped in swaddling clothes" (Luke 2:7). As a child, we are told, He "increased in wisdom and stature" (Luke 2:52). As a boy we find Him "asking questions" (Luke 2:46). As a man He was "wearied" in body (John 4:6). He was "a hungered" (Mat 4:2). He "slept" (Mar 4:38). He "marvelled" (Mar 6:6). He "wept" (John 11:35). He "prayed" (Mar 1:35). He "rejoiced" (Luke 10:21). He "groaned" (John 11:33). And here in our text He cried, "I thirst." That evidenced His humanity. God does not thirst. The angels do not. We shall not in glory "they shall hunger no more, neither thirst anymore" (Rev 7:16). But we thirst now because we are human and living in a world of sorrow. And Christ thirsted because He was man "Wherefore in all things it behooved him to be made like unto his brethren" (Heb 2:17).

"I thirst."

2. Here we see the intensity of Christ's sufferings. Let us first consider this cry of the Savior's as an expression of His bodily suffering. To realize something of what lay behind these words of His we must recall and review what preceded them. After instituting the Supper in the upper room, followed by the lengthy Pascal discourse to His apostles, the Redeemer adjourned to Gethsemane, and there for an hour He passed through the most excruciating agony. His soul was exceeding sorrowful. As He contemplated the awful cup, He shed not beads of perspiration but great drops of blood. His wrestling in the Garden was terminated by the appearing of the traitor accompanied by the band who had come to arrest Him. He was brought before

Caiaphas, and middle of the night though it was, He was examined and condemned. The Savior was held until early morning, and after the weary hours of waiting were over, was brought before Pilate. Following a lengthy trial, orders were given for Him to be scourged. Next, He was led, perhaps right across the city, to Herod's judgment-hall, and after a brief appearance before the Roman prelate, He was delivered into the hands of the brutal soldiers. Again, He was mocked and scourged, and again He was led across the city, back to Pilate. Once more there was the weary delay, the formalities of a trial, if such a farce deserves the name, followed by the passing of the sentence of death.

Then, with bleeding back, carrying His cross under the heat of the now almost-midday sun, He journeyed up the rugged heights of Golgotha. Reaching the appointed place of execution, His hands and feet were nailed to the tree. For three hours He hung there with the pitiless rays of the sun beating down on His thorn-crowned head. This was followed by three hours of darkness, now over. That night and that day were hours into which an eternity was compressed. Yet during it all, not a single word of murmuring passed His lips. There was no complaining, no begging for mercy. All His suffering had been borne in majestic silence. Like a sheep dumb before her shearers so He opened not His mouth. But now, at the end, His whole body wracked with pain, His mouth parched, He cries, "I thirst." It was not an appeal for pity, nor a request for the alleviation of His sufferings; it gave expression to the intensity of the agonies He was undergoing.

"I thirst." This was more than ordinary thirst. There was something deeper than physical sufferings behind it. A careful comparison of our text with Matthew 27:48 shows these words, "I thirst," followed on immediately after the fourth of our Savior's cross-utterances "Eli, Eli, lama, sabachthani" for while the soldier was pressing the sponge of vinegar to the sufferer's lips, some of the spectators cried out, "Let be, let us see whether Elijah will come to save him." We all know that the internal trials of the soul react upon the body, rending its nerves and affecting its strength "A broken spirit tries the bones" (Pro 17:22); "When I kept silence, my bones waxed old through my roaring all day long. For day and night your hand was heavy upon me: My moisture is turned into the drought of summer "(Psalm 32:3-4). The body and the soul sympathize with each other.

Let us remember that the Savior had just emerged from the three hours of darkness, during which God's face had been turned away from Him as He endured the fierceness of His out-poured wrath.

This cry of bodily suffering tells us, then, of the severity of the spiritual conflict through which He had just passed! Speaking anticipatively by the mouth of Jeremiah of this very hour, He said, "Is it nothing to you, all you that pass by? behold, and see if there be any sorrow like unto my sorrow, which is done upon me, with which the Lord has afflicted me in the day of his fierce anger. From above he has sent fire into my bones, and it prevails against them: He has spread a net for my feet, he has turned me back: he has made me desolate and faint "(Lam 1:12-13). His "thirst" was the effect of the agony of His soul in the fierce heat of God's wrath. It told of the drought of the land where the living God is not. But more: it plainly expressed His yearning for communion with God again, from Whom for three hours He had been separated. Was it not Christ Himself Who said by the spirit of prophecy, said it now, immediately He emerged from the darkness "As the deer pants after the water brooks, so pants my soul after you, O God; My soul thirsts for God, for the living God: when shall I come and appear before God!" Do not the words which follow identify the Speaker and reveal the time that longing and "panting was expressed" "My tears have been my meat day and night, while they continually say unto me, Where is your God?" (Psalm 42:1-3).

"I thirst."

3. Here we see our Lord's deep reverence for the Scriptures. How constantly the Savior's mind turned toward the sacred oracles! He lived indeed by every word that proceeds out of the mouth of

God. He was the "blessed man" that meditated in God's Law "day and night" (Psalm 1). The written Word was that which formed His thoughts, filled His heart, and regulated His ways. The Scriptures are the transcript of the Father's will, and that was ever His delight. In the temptation, that which was written was His defence. In His teaching, the statutes of the Lord were His authority. In His controversies with the scribes and Pharisees, His appeal was ever to the Law and the Testimony. And now, in His death-hour His mind dwelt upon the Word of Truth.

In order to get the primary force of this fifth Cross-utterance of the Savior, we must note its setting: "Jesus knowing that all things were now accomplished, that the scripture might be fulfilled, says, I thirst" (John 19:28). The reference is to the Sixty-ninth Psalm another of the Messianic Psalms which describes so graphically His passion. In it the Spirit of prophecy had declared, "They gave me also gall for my meat; and in my thirst they gave me vinegar to drink" (vs. 21). This remained yet unaccomplished. The predictions of the previous verses had already received fulfilment. He had sunk in the "deep mire" (vs. 2); He had been "hated without a cause" (vs. 4); He had "borne reproach and shame" (vs. 7); He had "become a stranger unto his brethren" (vs. 8); He had become "a proverb" to His revilers, and "the song of the drunkards" (vss. 11-12); He had "cried unto God" in His distress (vss. 16-20) and now there remained nothing more than the offering Him the drink of vinegar and gall, and in order to this He cried,

"I thirst."

"Jesus knowing that ALL things were now accomplished, that the scripture might be fulfilled, says, I thirst." How completely self-possessed the Savior was! He had hung on that Cross for six hours and had passed through unparalleled suffering yet is His mind clear and His memory unimpaired. He had before Him, with perfect distinctness, the whole truth of God. He reviewed the entire scope of Messianic prediction. He remembers there is one prophetic Scripture unaccomplished. He overlooked nothing. What proof is this that He was divinely superior to all circumstances!

Before passing on, we would briefly point an application to ourselves. We have remarked how the Savior bowed to the authority of Scripture both in life and death, Christian reader, how is it with you? Is the Book divine the final court of appeal with you? Do you discover in its revelation of God's mind and will concerning you? Is it a lamp unto your feet? that is, are you walking in its light? Are its commands binding on you? Are you really obeying it? Can you say with David, "I have chosen the way of truth: your judgments have I laid before me? I have stuck unto your testimonies...I thought on my ways and turned my feet unto your testimonies. I made haste, and delayed not to keep your commandments" (Psalm 119:30-31, 59, 70)? Are you, like the Savior, anxious to fulfil the Scriptures? O may writer and reader seek grace to pray from the heart, "Make me to go in the path of your commandments; for therein do I delight. Incline my heart unto your testimonies...Order my steps in your word: and let not any iniquity have dominion over me" (Psalm 119:35, 36, 133).

"I thirst."

4. Here we see the Savior's submission to the Father's will. The Savior thirsted, and He who thirsted thus, remember, possessed all power in Heaven and earth. Had He chosen to exercise His omnipotency, He could have readily satisfied His need. He who of old had caused the water to flow from the smitten rock for the refreshment of Israel in the wilderness, had the same infinite resources at His disposal now. He who turned the water into wine at a word, could have spoken the word of power here, and met His own need. But He never once performed a miracle for His own benefit or comfort. When tempted by Satan to do this, He refused. Why did He now decline to satisfy His pressing need? Why hang there on the Cross with parched lips? Because in the volume of the Book which expressed God's will, it was written that He should thirst, and that thirsting He should be "given" vinegar to drink. And He came here to do God's will, and therefore

did He submit.

In death, as in life, Scripture was for the Lord Jesus the authoritative Word of the living God. In the temptation He had refused to minister to His need apart from that Word by which He lived, and so now He makes known His need, not that it might be ministered unto, but that Scripture might be fulfilled. Mark: He does not Himself fulfil it; God can be trusted to take care of that; but He gives utterance to His distress so as to provide occasion for the fulfilment. As another has said, "The terrible thirst of crucifixion is upon Him, but that is not enough to force those parched lips to speak; but it is written; 'In My thirst they gave Me vinegar to drink' this opens them" (F.W. Grant).

Here then, as ever, He shows Himself in active obedience to the will of God, which He came to accomplish. He simply says, "I thirst"; the vinegar is offered, and the prophecy is fulfilled. What perfect absorption in His Father's will!

Again, we pause to point an application to ourselves, a double one. First, the Lord Jesus delighted in the Father's will even when it involved the suffering of thirst. Are we so resigned to Him? Have we sought grace to say, "Not my will, but your, be done?" Can we exclaim "even so, Father, for so it seemed good in your sight?" Have we learned in whatever state we are in "therewith to be content "(Phi 4:11)? But now mark a contrast. The Son of God was denied a draught of cold water to relieve His suffering how different with us! God has given us a variety of refreshments to relieve us, yet how often are we unthankful! We have better things than a cup of water to delight us when thirsty yet are we not grateful. O if this cry of Christ's were but believingly considered, it would make us bless God for what we now almost despise and beget contentment in us for the most common mercies. Did the Lord of Glory cry "I thirst" and had nothing in His extremity to comfort Him, and do you, who have a thousand times forfeited all right to temporal as well as spiritual mercies, slight the common bounties of providence! What! grumble at a cup of water, who deserved but a cup of wrath. O lay it to heart and learn to be contented with what you have, though it be but the very barest necessities of life. Complain not if you dwell in but a humble hovel, for your Savior had not where to lay His head! Complain not if you have nothing but bread to eat, for your Savior lacked that for forty days! Complain not if you have only water to drink, for your Savior was denied even that in the hour of death!

"I thirst."

5. Here we see how Christ can sympathize with His suffering people. The problem of suffering has ever been a perplexing one. Why should suffering be necessary in a world that is governed by a perfect God? a God Who not only has the power to prevent evil, but Who is Love.

Why should there be pain and wretchedness, sickness, and death? As we look out on the world and take cognizance of its countless sufferers, we are bewildered. This world is but a Valley of Tears. A thin veneer of gaiety scarcely succeeds in hiding the drab facts of life. Philosophizing about the problem of suffering brings scant relief. After all our reasonings we ask, Does God, see? Is there knowledge with the Highest? Does He really care? Like all questions, these must be taken to the Cross. While they do not find there a complete answer, nevertheless they do meet that which satisfies the anxious heart. While the problem of suffering is not fully solved there, yet the Cross does throw sufficient light upon it to relieve the tension. The Cross shows us that God is not ignorant of our sorrows, for in the person of His Son He has Himself "borne our griefs and carried our sorrows" (Isa 53:4)! The Cross shows us God is not unmindful of our distress and anguish, for becoming incarnate He suffered Himself! The Cross tells us God is not indifferent to pain, for in the Savior, He experienced it!

What then is the value of these facts? This: "For we have not a high priest which cannot be touched with the feeling of our infirmities; but was in all points tempted [or tried] like as we are, yet without sin" (Heb 4:15). Our Redeemer is not one so removed from us that

He is unable to enter, sympathetically, into our sorrows, for He was Himself "The man of sorrows."

Here then is comfort for the aching heart. No matter how despondent you may be, no matter how rugged your path and sad your lot, you are invited to spread it all before the Lord Jesus and cast all your care upon Him, knowing that "He cares for you" (1 Peter 5:7). Is your body wracked with pain? So was His! Are you misunderstood, misjudged, misrepresented? So was He! Have those who are nearest and dearest turned away from you? They did from Him! Are you in the darkness? So was He for three hours! "Wherefore in all things it behooved him to be made like unto his brethren, that he might be a merciful and faithful high priest" (Heb 2:17).

"I thirst."

6. Here we see the expression of a universal need. Whether he articulates it or not, the natural man the world over is crying, "I thirst." Why this consuming desire to acquire wealth? Why this craving for the honours and plaudits of the world? Why this mad rush after pleasure, the turning from one form of it to another with persistent and unwearied diligence? Why this eager search for wisdom this scientific inquiry, this pursuit of philosophy, this ransacking of the writings of the ancients, and this ceaseless experimentation by the moderns? Why the insane craze for that which is novel? Why? Because there is an aching void in the soul. Because there is something remaining in every natural man that is unsatisfied. This is true of the millionaire equally as much as the pauper: the riches of the former bring no real contentment. It is as true of the globe-trotter equally as much as of the country rustic who has never been outside the bounds of his native country: traveling from one end of the earth to the other and back again, fails to discover the secret of peace. Over all the cisterns of this world's providing is written in letters of ineffaceable truth, "Whoever drinks of this water shall thirst again" (John 4:13). So, it is also with the religious man or woman: we mean, the religious without Christ. How many there are who go

the weary round of religious performances and find nothing to meet their deep need! They are members of an evangelical denomination; they attend church regularly, contribute of their means to the pastor's support, read their Bibles occasionally, and sometimes pray, or, if they use a "prayer-book," say their prayers every night. And yet, after it all if they are honest, their cry is still

"I thirst."

The thirst is a spiritual one: that is why natural things cannot quench it. Unknown to themselves, their soul "thirsts for God" (Psalm 42:2). God made us, and He alone can satisfy us. Said the Lord Jesus, "Whoever drinks of the water that I shall give him shall never thirst" (John 4:14). Christ alone can quench our thirst. He alone can meet the deep need of our hearts. He alone can impart that peace which the world knows nothing of and can neither bestow nor take away. O reader, once more I would address myself to your conscience. How is it with you? Have you found that everything under the sun is only vanity and vexation of spirit? Have you discovered that the things of earth are unable to satisfy your heart? Is your soul-cry "I thirst"? Then, is it not good news to hear there is One who can satisfy you? One we say, not a creed, not a form of religion, but a person, a living, divine person. He it is who says, "Come unto me, all you that labour and are heavy-laden, and I will give you rest" (Mat 11:28). Heed then that sweet invitation. Come to Him now, just as you are. Come in faith, believing He will receive you; and then shall you sing

"I came to Jesus as I was,

Weary, and worn, and sad,

I found in Him a resting place,

And He has made me glad."

O come to Christ. Delay not. You are "thirsty"? then you are the one He is seeking for: "Blessed are they which do hunger and thirst after righteousness: for they shall be filled" (Mat 5:6).

Unsaved reader, reject not the Savior, for if you die in your sins your eternal cry will be, "I thirst!" This is the moan of the damned. In the Lake of Fire, the lost suffer amid the flames of God's wrath forever and ever. If Christ cried "I thirst" when He suffered the wrath of God for but three hours, what is the state of those who have to endure it for all eternity! When millions of years have gone, ten millions more lie ahead. There is an everlasting thirst in Hell which admits of no relief. Remember the awful words of the rich man: "And he cried, and said, Father Abraham, have mercy on me, and send Lazarus that he may dip the tip of his finger in water, and cool my tongue; for I am tormented in this flame" (Luke 16:24). O think, my reader. If physical thirst in the extreme is insufferable even now when endured but a few short hours, what will that thirst be which is infinitely beyond any present thirst, and which shall never be quenched! Say not it is cruel of God to deal thus with His erring creatures.

Remember to what He exposed His own dear Son, when sin was imputed to Him surely the one who despises Christ is deserving of the hottest place in Hell! Again, we say, Receive Him now as yours. Receive Him as your Savior and submit to Him as your Lord.

"I thirst."

7. Here we see the enunciation of an abiding principle. There is a sense, a real one, in which Christ still thirsts. He is thirsting for the love and devotion of His own. He is yearning for fellowship with His blood-bought people. Here is one of the great marvels of grace, a redeemed sinner can offer that which satisfies the heart of Christ! I can understand how I ought to appreciate His love, but how wonderful that He, the all-sufficient One should appreciate my love! I have learned how blessed to my own soul is communion with Him, but who would have supposed that my communion was blessed to Christ! Yet it is. For this He still "thirsts." Grace enables us to offer that which refreshes Him. Wondrous thought!

Have you ever noticed in John 4 that though Christ said to the woman who came to the well, "Give me to drink" for He sat there "wearied" from the journey and heat that He never took a drink of water? In the salvation and faith of that Samaritan woman He found that which refreshed His heart! Love is never satisfied until there is a response and love in return! So, with Christ. Here is the key to Revelation 3:20 "Behold, I stand at the door, and knock: if any man hear my voice, and open the door, I will come into him, and will sup with him, and he with me." This is often applied to the unsaved, but its primary reference is to the Church. It pictures Christ seeking the fellowship of His own. He speaks of "supping" and in Scripture supping is ever symbolic of communion, just as the Lord's Supper is a special season of communion between the Savior and the saved. And observe in this passage Christ speaks of a double supping "I will come into him, and sup with him and he with me." Not only is it our unspeakable privilege to sup with Him, and to commune with Him, to delight ourselves in Him, but He sups with us. He finds in our communion something for His heart to feed upon, something which refreshes Him, and that something is our devotion and love. Yes, the Christ of God still "thirsts," thirsts for the affection of His own. O will you not offer that which will satisfy Him? Respond then to His own call "Set me as a seal upon your heart" (Song 8:6).6

5 The last half of the first verse of the hymn "I Heard the Voice of Jesus Say" by Horatius Bonar (1808-1889). The second verse explains why He makes us glad: "I heard the voice of Jesus say, 'Behold I freely give The living water, thirsty one, Stoop down, and drink, and live.' I came to Jesus, and I drank of that life-giving stream; My thirst was quenched, my soul revived, and now I live in Him." 6 Cecil Frances Alexander's (1823-1895) hymn is most appropriate: His are the thousand sparkling rills That from a thousand fountains burst, And fill with music all the hills; And yet He says, "I thirst." All fiery pangs on battle fields, On fever beds where sick men toss, Are in that human cry He yields, To anguish on the Cross.

6. The Word Of Victory

"When Jesus therefore had received the vinegar, he said, It is finished." John 19:30

Our last two studies have been occupied with the tragedy of the Cross we turn now to its triumph. In His words, "My God, my God, why have you forsaken me?" we heard the Savior's cry of desolation. In His words, "I thirst" we listened to His cry of lamentation. Now there falls upon our ears His cry of jubilation "It is finished." From the words of the victim, we turn now to the words of the victor. It is proverbial that every cloud has its silver lining: so, had the darkest cloud of all. The Cross of Christ has two great sides to it: it showed the profound depths of His humiliation, but it also marked the goal of the Incarnation, and further, it told the consummation of His mission, and it forms the basis of our salvation.

"It is finished." The ancient Greeks boasted of being able to say much in little "to give a sea of matter in a drop of language" was regarded as the perfection of oratory. What they sought is here found. "It is finished" is but one word in the original, yet in that word is wrapped up the Gospel of God. In that word is contained the ground of the believer's assurance. In that word is discovered the sum of all joy, and the very spirit of all divine consolation.

"It is finished." This was not the despairing cry of a helpless martyr. It was not an expression of satisfaction that the termination of His sufferings was now reached. It was not the last gasp of a worn-out life. No, rather was it the declaration on the part of the divine Redeemer that all for which He came from Heaven to earth to do, was now done; that all that was needed to reveal the full character of God had now been accomplished; that all that was required by the Law before sinners could be saved, had now been performed that the full price of our redemption was now paid.

"It is finished." The great purpose of God in the history of man was now accomplished de jure as it will yet be de facto. From the beginning, God's purpose has always been one and indivisible. It had been declared to men in various ways: in symbol and type, by mysterious hints and by plain intimations, through Messianic prediction and through didactic declaration. That purpose of God may be summarized thus: to display His grace and to magnify His Son in the creating of children in His own image and glory. And at the Cross the foundation was laid which was to make this possible and actual.

"It is finished." What was finished? The answer to this question is a very full one, though a number of excellent expositors have sought to limit the scope of these words and to confine them strictly to a single application. We are told it was the prophecies concerning the sufferings of the Savior which were finished, and that He referred only to this. It is readily granted that the immediate reference was to the Messianic predictions, yet we think there are good and sufficient reasons for not confining our Lord's words here to them. Yes, to us it seems certain that Christ referred specially to His sacrificial work, for all Scripture concerning His suffering and shame was not yet fulfilled. There still remained the dismissal of His spirit into the hands of the Father (Psalm 31:5); there still remained the "piercing" with the spear (Zechariah 12:10: and note that the word used in Psalm 22:16 for the piercing of His hands and feet, the act of crucifixion is a different one); there still remained the preserving of His bones unbroken (Psalm 34:20), and the burial in the rich man's grave (Isa 53:9).

"It is finished." What was finished? We answer, His sacrificial work. It is true there yet remained the act of death itself, which was necessary for the making of atonement. But as is so often the case here in John's Gospel wherein our text is found (cf. John 12:23, 31; 13:31; 16:5; 17:4), the Lord here speaks anticipatively of the completion of His work. Moreover, it must be remembered that the three hours darkness was already past, the awful cup had already been drained, His precious blood had already been shed, the outpoured wrath of God had already been endured; and these are the primary elements in the making of atoning sacrifice. The sacrificial work of the Savior, then, was completed, excepting only the act of death which followed immediately. But, as we shall see, the completing of the sacrificial work made an end of a number of things, and to them we shall now turn our attention.

"It is finished."

1. Here we see the accomplished fulfilment of all the prophecies which had been written of Him before He should die. This is the immediate thought of the context: "When Jesus therefore had received the vinegar, He said, It is finished" (John 19:30). Centuries beforehand, the prophets of God had described step by step the humiliation and suffering which the coming Savior should undergo. One by one these had been fulfilled, wonderfully fulfilled, fulfilled to the very letter. Had prophecy declared that He should be the "woman's seed" (Gen 3:15), then He was "born of a woman" (Gal 4:4). Had prophecy announced that His mother should be a "virgin" (Isa 7:14), then was it literally fulfilled (Mat 1:18). Had prophecy revealed that He should be of the seed of Abraham (Gen 22:18), then mark its fulfilment (Mat 1:1). Had prophecy made it known that He should be a lineal descendant of David (2 Samuel 7:12-13), then such He actually was (Rom 1:3). Had prophecy said that He should be named before He was born (Isa 49:1), then so it came to pass (Luke 1:30-31). Had prophecy foretold that He should be born in Bethlehem of Judea (Mic 5:2), then mark how this very village was actually His birthplace.

Had prophecy forewarned that His birth should entail sorrowing for others (Jer 31:15), then behold its tragic fulfilment (Mat 2:14-18). Had prophecy foreshown that the Messiah should appear before the sceptre of tribal ascendancy had departed from Judah (Gen 49:10), then so He did, for though the ten tribes were in captivity, Judah was still in the land at the time of His advent. Had prophecy referred to the flight into Egypt and the subsequent return into Palestine (Hos 11:1 and cf. Isa 49:3, 6), then so it came to pass (Mat 2:1415).

Had prophecy made mention of one going before Christ to make ready His way (Mal 3:1), then see its fulfilment in the person of John the Baptist. Had prophecy made it known that at the Messiah's appearing "the eyes of the blind shall be opened, and the ears of the deaf shall be unstopped, then shall the lame man leap as a deer, and the tongue of the dumb sing" (Isa 35:56), then read through the four Gospels and see how blessedly this proved true. Had prophecy spoken of Him as "poor and needy" (Psalm 40:17, see beginning of Psalm), then behold Him not having where to lay His head. Had prophecy intimated that He should speak in "parables" (Psalm 78:2), then such was frequently His method of teaching. Had prophecy depicted Him stilling the tempest (Psalm 107:29), then this is exactly what He did. Had prophecy heralded His "triumphal entry" into Jerusalem (Zechariah 9:9), then so it came to pass!

Had prophecy announced that His person should be despised (Isa 53:3), that He should be rejected by the Jews (Isa 8:14), that He should be "hated without a cause" (Psalm 69:4), then sad to say, such was precisely the case. Had prophecy painted the whole picture of His degradation and crucifixion, then was it vividly reproduced. There had been the betrayal by a familiar friend, the forsaking by His cherished disciples, the being led to the slaughter, the being taken to judgment, the appearing of false witnesses against Him, the refusal on His part to make defence, the establishing of His innocence, the unjust condemnation, the sentence of capital punishment passed upon Him, the literal piercing of His hands and feet, the being numbered with transgressors, the mockery of the crowd, the casting lots for His garments all predicted centuries beforehand, and all fulfilled to the very letter. The last prophecy of all which remained before He committed His Spirit into the hands of His Father, had now been fulfilled. He cried "I thirst," and after the tendering of the vinegar and gall, all was now "accomplished" and as the Lord Jesus reviewed the entire scope of the prophetic Word and saw its full realization, He cried, "It is finished"!

It only remains for us to point out that as there was a complete set of prophecies which had to do with the first advent of the Savior, so also is there a complete set of prophecies which have to do with His second advent, the latter as definite, as personal, and as comprehensive in their scope as the former. As then we see the actual fulfilment of those which had to do with His first coming to the earth, we may look forward with absolute confidence and assurance to the fulfilment of those which have to do with His second coming. And, as we have seen that the former set of prophecies were fulfilled literally, actually, personally, so also must we expect the latter set to be. To grant the literal fulfilment of the former, and then to seek to spiritualize and symbolize the latter, is not only grossly inconsistent and illogical, but is highly injurious to us and deeply dishonouring to God and to His Word.

"It is finished."

2. Here we see the completion of His sufferings. But what tongue or pen can describe the sufferings of the Savior? O the unutterable anguish, physical, mental, and spiritual, which He endured! Appropriately was He designated "the man of sorrows": suffering at the hands of men, at the hands of Satan, and at the hands of God. Pain inflicted upon Him by enemies and friends alike. From the beginning He walked amid the shadows which the Cross cast athwart His path. Hear His lament: "I am afflicted and ready to die from my youth up" (Psalm 88:15). What a light this throws on His earlier years! Who can say how much is contained in those words? For us, an impenetrable

veil is cast over the future; none of us knows what a day may bring forth.

But the Savior knew the end from the beginning! One has only to read through the Gospels to learn how the awful Cross was ever before Him. At the marriage-feast of Cana, where all was gladness and merriment, He makes solemn reference to "his hour" not yet come. When Nicodemus interviewed Him at night, the Savior referred to the "lifting up of the Son of man." When James and John came to request from Him the two places of honour in His coming kingdom, He made mention of the "cup" which He had to drink, and of the "baptism" with which He must be baptized. When Peter confessed that He was the Christ, the Son of the living God, He turned to His disciples and began to show unto them "how that he must go unto Jerusalem and suffer many things of the elders and chief priests and scribes, and be killed, and be raised again the third day" (Mat 16:21). When Moses and Elijah stood with Him on the Mount of Transfiguration, it was to speak of "his decease which he should accomplish at Jerusalem" (Luke 9:31).

If it is true, we are quite unable to estimate the sufferings of Christ due to the anticipation of the Cross, still less can we fathom the dread reality itself. The physical sufferings were excruciating, but even this was as nothing compared with His anguish of soul. To a consideration of these sufferings, we have already devoted several paragraphs in previous chapters, yet we make no apology in turning to them again. We cannot contemplate too often what the Savior endured in order to secure our salvation. The better we are acquainted with His sufferings, and the more frequently we meditate thereon, the warmer will be our love and the deeper our gratitude.

At last, the closing hours have come. There had been the terrible experience in Gethsemane followed by the appearing's before Caiaphas, before Pilate, before Herod, and back again before Pilate. There had been the scourging and mocking by the brutal soldiers; the journey to Calvary; the fastening of His hands and feet to the cruel tree. There had been the reviling of the priests, the crowd, and the two thieves crucified with Him. There had been the callous indifference of a vulgar mob, among whom "none took pity" and none spoke a word of "comfort" (Psalm 69:20). There had been the awful cloud that hid from the Father's face, which wrung from Him the bitter cry, "My God, my God, why have you forsaken me?" There had been the parched lips which drew from Him the exclamation "I thirst." There had been the fearful conflict with the power of darkness as the serpent "bruised" His heel. Well might the Sufferer ask, "Is it nothing to you, all you that pass by? behold, and see if there be any sorrow like unto my sorrow, which is done unto me, with which the Lord has afflicted me in the day of his fierce anger" (Lam 1:12).

But now the suffering is ended. That from which His holy soul shrank is over. The Lord has bruised Him man and Devil have done their worst. The cup has been drained. The awful storm of God's wrath has spent itself. The darkness is ended. The sword of divine justice is sheathed. The wages of sin have been paid. The prophecies of His sufferings are all fulfilled. The Cross has been "endured." Divine holiness has been fully satisfied (Isa 53:11). With a cry of triumph, a loud cry, a cry which reverberated throughout the entire universe the Savior exclaims, "It is finished." The ignominy and shame, the suffering and agony, are past. Never again shall He experience pain. Never again shall He endure the contradiction of sinners against Himself. Never again shall He be in the hands of Satan. Never again shall the light of God's countenance be hidden from Him. Blessed be God, all that is finished! "It is finished."

3. Here we see the goal of the incarnation is reached. Scripture indicates there is a special work peculiar to each of the divine Persons; though, like the Persons themselves, it is not always easy to distinguish between Their respective works. God the Father is especially concerned in the government of the world: He rules over all the works of His hands. God the Son is especially concerned in the work of Redemption: He was the One who came here to die for

sinners. God the Spirit is especially concerned with the Scriptures: He was the One who moved holy men of old to speak the messages of God, as He is the One who now gives spiritual illumination and understanding, and guides into the truth. But it is with the work of God the Son we are here particularly concerned.

Before the Lord Jesus came to this earth, a definite work was committed to Him. In the volume of the book, it was written of Him, and He came to do the recorded will of God. Even as a boy of twelve the "Father's business" was before His heart and occupied His attention. Again, in John 5:36 we find Him saying, "But I have greater witness than that of John: for the works which the Father has given me to finish, the same works that I do." And on the last night before His death, in that wonderful high priestly prayer, we find Him saying, "I have glorified you on the earth: I have finished the work which you gave me to do" (John 17:4).

In his book on the Seven Sayings of Christ on the Cross, Dr. Anderson-Berry makes use of an illustration from history which by its striking antithesis shows up the meaning and glory of the finished work of Christ. Elizabeth, the Queen of England, the idol of society and the leader of European fashion, when on her deathbed turned to her lady in waiting, and said, "O my God! It is over. I have come to the end of it—the end, the end. To have only one life, and to have done with it! To have lived, and loved, and triumphed; and now to know it is over! One may defy everything else but this." And as the listener sat watching, in a few moments more the face whose slightest smile had brought her courtiers to their feet, turned into a mask of lifeless clay, and returned the anxious gaze of her servant with nothing more than a vacant stare. Such was the end of one whose meteoric course had been the envy of half the world. It could not be said that she had "finished" anything, for with her all was "vanity and vexation of spirit." How different with the end of the Savior! "I have glorified you on earth: I have finished the work which you gave me to do."

The mission upon which God had sent His Son into the world was now accomplished. It was not actually finished until He breathed His last, but death was only an instant ahead, and in anticipation of it He cries "It is finished." The difficult work is done. The divinely given task is performed. A work more honourable and momentous than ever entrusted to man or angels, has been completed. That for which He had left Heaven's glory, that for which He had taken upon Him the form of a servant, that for which He had remained upon earth for thirty-three years to do, was now consummated. Nothing remained to be added. The goal of the Incarnation is reached. With what joyous triumph must He here have viewed the arduous and costly work which, committed to Him, had now been perfected!

"It is finished." The mission upon which God had sent His Son into the world was accomplished. That which had been eternally purposed had come to pass. The plan of God had been fully carried out. It is true that the Savior had been by "wicked hands crucified and slain," yet was He "delivered by the determinate counsel and foreknowledge of God" (Act 2:23). It is true that the kings of the earth stood up, and the rulers were gathered together against the Lord, and against His Christ nevertheless it was but for to do what God's hand and God's counsel "determined before to be done" (Act 4:28). Because He is the Highest, God's will cannot be thwarted. Because He is supreme, God's counsel must stand. Because He is almighty, God's purpose cannot be overthrown.

Again, and again the Scriptures insist upon the irresistibility of the pleasure of the Lord God. Because this truth is now so generally called into question, we subjoin seven passages which affirm it: "But he is in one mind, and who can turn him? and what his soul desires, even that he does" (Job 23:13). "I know that you can do everything, and that no thought can be withheld from you" (Job 42:2). "But our God is in the heavens: He has done whatever he has pleased "(Psalm 115:3). "There is no wisdom nor understanding nor counsel against the Lord "(Pro 21:30). "For the Lord of hosts has purposed, and who shall disannul it? and His hand is stretched out, and who shall turn it back?" (Isa 14:27). "Remember the former things of old: for I am God, and there is none else; I am God, and there is none like me: Declaring the end from the beginning, and from ancient times the things that are not yet done, saying, My counsel shall stand, and I will do all my pleasure" (Isa 46:9-10). "And all the inhabitants of the earth are reputed as nothing: and he does according to his will in the army of Heaven, and among the inhabitants of the earth: and none can stay his hand, or say unto him, What do you?" (Dan 4:35). And, in the triumphant cry of the Savior "It is finished" we have a prophecy and pledge of the ultimate carrying out of God's plan completely and irresistibly. At the end of time, when everything is wound up, and God's purpose has been fully consummated, when everything has been done which, He before determined should be done, then shall it be said again, "It is finished."

"It is finished."

4. Here we see the accomplishment of the Atonement. Above we have spoken of Christ reaching the goal of the Incarnation, and of the consummation of His mission to the earth; what that goal and mission was, the Scriptures plainly reveal. The Son of Man came here "to seek and to save that which was lost" (Luke 19:10). Christ Jesus came into the world "to save sinners" (1 Timothy 1:15). God sent forth His Son, born of a woman, "to redeem them that were under the law" (Gal 4:5). He was manifested "to take away our sins" (1 John 3:5). And all this involved the Cross. The "lost" which He came to seek could only be found there in the place of death and under the condemnation of God. Sinners could be "saved" only by One taking their place and bearing their iniquities. They who were under the Law could be "redeemed" only by Another fulfilling its requirements and suffering its curse. Our sins could be "taken away" only by their being blotted out by the precious blood of Christ. The demands of justice must be met; the requirements of God's holiness must be satisfied; the awful debt we incurred must be paid. And on the Cross, this was done; done by none less than the Son of God; done perfectly; done

once for all. "It is finished."

That to which so many types looked forward, that which so much in the Tabernacle and its ritual foreshadowed, that of which so many of God's prophets had spoken, was now accomplished. A covering from sin and its shame, typified by the coats of skin with which the Lord God clothed our first parents, was now provided. The more excellent sacrifice, typified by Abel's lamb, had now been offered. A shelter from the storm of divine judgment, typified by the Ark of Noah, was now furnished. The only begotten and well-beloved Son, typified by Abraham's offering up of Isaac, had already been placed upon the altar. A protection from the avenging angel, typified by the shed blood of the Passover-lamb, was now supplied. A cure from the serpent's bite, typified by the serpent of brass upon the pole, was now made ready for sinners. The providing of a life-giving fountain, typified by Moses striking the rock, was now affected.

"It is finished." The Greek word here, teleo, is translated variously in the New Testament. A glance at some of the different renderings in other passages will enable us to discern the fullness and finality of the term used by the Savior. In Matthew 11:1, teleo is rendered as follows, "When Jesus had made an end of commanding his twelve disciples, he departed thence." In Matthew 17:24 it is rendered, "They that received tribute money came to Peter, and said, Does not your master pay tribute?" In Luke 2:39, it is rendered, "And when they had performed all things according to the Law of the Lord, they returned into Galilee." In Luke 18:31, it is rendered, "All things that are written by the prophets concerning the Son shall be accomplished."

Putting these together we learn the scope of the Savior's sixth Cross-utterance. "It is finished." He cried: it is "made an end of"; it is "paid"; it is "performed"; it is "accomplished." What was made an end of? our sins and their guilt. What was "paid?" the price of our redemption. What was "performed?" the utmost requirements of the Law. What was "accomplished?" the work which the Father had given Him to do. What was "finished?" the making of atonement.

God has furnished at least four proofs that Christ did finish the work which was given Him to do. First, in the rending of the veil, which showed that the way to God was now open. Second, in the raising of Christ from the dead, which evidenced that God had accepted His sacrifice. Third, the exaltation of Christ to His own right hand, which demonstrated the value of Christ's work and the Father's delight in His person. Fourth, the sending to earth of the Holy Spirit to apply the virtues and benefits of Christ's atoning death.

"It is finished." What was "finished?" the work of atonement. What is the value of that to us? This to the sinner, it is a message of glad tidings. All that a holy God requires has been done. Nothing is left for the sinner to add. No works from us are demanded as the price of our salvation. All that is necessary for the sinner is to rest now by faith upon what Christ did. "The gift of God is eternal life through Jesus Christ our Lord" (Rom 6:23). To the believer, the knowledge that the atoning work of Christ is finished brings a sweet relief over against all the defects and imperfections of his services. There is nothing "finished" that we do: all our duties are imperfect. There is much of sin and vanity in the very best of our efforts, but the grand relief is that we are "complete" in Christ (Col 2:10)! Christ and His finished work are the ground of all our hopes. "It is finished."

"Upon a Life I did not live,

Upon a Death I did not die,

Another's death

Another's life I cast my soul eternally.

Bold, shall I stand in that great day,

For whom, anything to my charge can lay?

Fully absolved by Christ I am,

From sin's tremendous curse and blame."

5. Here we see the end of our sins. The sins of the believer, all of them, were transferred to the Savior. As says the Scripture, "The Lord has laid on him the iniquities of us all" (Isa 53:6). If then God laid my iniquities on Christ, they are no longer on me. Sin there is in me, for the old Adamic nature remains in the believer until death or until Christ's return, should He come before I die; but there is no sin on me. This distinction between sin in and sin on, is a vital one, and there should be little difficulty in apprehending it. Where I to say the judge passed sentence on a criminal, and that he is now under sentence of death, everyone would understand what I meant. In like manner, everyone out of Christ has the sentence of God's condemnation resting upon him. But when a sinner believes in the Lord Jesus, receives Him as his Lord and Master, he is no longer "under condemnation" sin is no longer on him, that is, the guilt, the condemnation, the penalty of sin, is no longer upon him. And why? Because Christ bore our sins in His own body on the tree (1 Peter 2:24) the guilt, condemnation, and penalty of our sins, was transferred to our substitute. Hence, because my sins were transferred to Christ, they are no more upon me.

This precious truth was strikingly illustrated in Old Testament times in connection with Israel's annual Day of Atonement. On that day, Aaron, the high priest (a type of Christ), made satisfaction to God for the sins which Israel had committed during the previous year. The manner in which this was done is described in Leviticus 16. Two goats were taken and presented before the Lord at the door of the tabernacle: this was before anything was done with them: it represented Christ presenting Himself to God, offering to come into this world and be the Savior of sinners. One of the goats was then taken and killed, and its blood was carried into the tabernacle, within the veil, into the Holy of Holies, and there it was sprinkled before and upon the mercy seat foreshadowing Christ offering Himself as a sacrifice to God, to meet the demands of His justice and satisfy the requirements of His holiness.

Then we read that Aaron came out of the tabernacle and laid both his hands upon the head of the second (living) goat signifying an act of identification by which Aaron is the representative of the whole nation, identified the people with it, acknowledging that its doom was what their sins merited, and which, today, corresponds with the hands of faith laying hold of Christ and identifying ourselves with Him in His Death. Having laid his hands on the head of the live goat, Aaron now confessed over him "all the iniquities of the children of Israel, and all their transgressions in all their sins, putting them upon the head of the goat" (Lev 16:21). Thus were Israel's sins transferred to their substitute. Finally, we are told, "And the goat shall bear upon him all their iniquities unto a land not inhabited: and he shall let go the goat in the wilderness" (Lev 16:22). The goat bearing Israel's sins, was taken unto an uninhabited wilderness, and the people of God saw him and their sins no more! In type this was Christ taking our sins into that desolate land where God was not, and there making an end of them. The Cross of Christ then is the grave of our sins!

"It is finished."

6. Here we see the fulfilment of the Law's requirements. "The law is holy, and the commandment holy, and just and good" (Rom 7:12). How could it be anything less when Jehovah Himself had framed and given it! The fault lay not in the Law but in man who, being depraved and sinful, could not keep it. Yet that Law must be kept, and kept by a man, so that the Law might be honoured and magnified, and its giver vindicated. Therefore, we read "For what the law could not do, in that it was weak through the flesh, God sending his own Son, in the likeness of sinful flesh, and for sin, condemned sin in the flesh: that the righteousness of the law might be fulfilled in (not by) us, who walk not after flesh, but after the Spirit" (Rom 8:3-4). The "weakness" here is that of fallen man. The sending forth of God's Son in the likeness of sin's flesh (Greek) refers to the Incarnation: as we read in another Scripture, "God sent forth his Son, born of a woman, born under the law, that he might redeem them that were under the

law" (Gal 4:4-5 RV). Yes, the Savior was born "under the law," born under it that He might keep it perfectly in thought, word, and deed. "Think not that I am come to destroy the law, or the prophets: I am not come to destroy, but to fulfil "(Mat 5:17); such was His claim.

But not only did the Savior keep the precepts of the Law, but He also suffered its penalty and endured its curse. We had broken it, and taking our place, He must receive its just sentence. Having received its penalty and endured its curse, the demands of the Law are fully met, and justice is satisfied. Therefore, is it written of believers, "Christ has redeemed us from the curse of the law, being made a curse for us" (Gal 3:13). And again, "For Christ is the end of the law for righteousness to everyone that believes" (Rom 10:4). And yet again, "For you are not under the law, but under grace" (Rom 6:14). "It is finished."

"Free from the Law, O happy condition!

Jesus has bled, and there is remission,

Cursed by the law and bruised by the fall,

Grace has redeemed us once for all."

7. Here we see the destruction of Satan's power. See it by faith. The Cross sounded the death-knell of the devil's power. To human appearances it looked like the moment of his greatest triumph, yet in reality, it was the hour of his ultimate defeat. In view of the Cross (see context) the Savior declared, "Now is the judgment of this world: now shall the prince of this world be cast out" (John 12:31). It is true that Satan has not yet been chained and cast into the bottomless pit, nevertheless, sentence has been passed (though not yet executed) his doom is certain; and his power is already broken so far as believers are concerned.

For the Christian, the devil is a vanquished foe. He was defeated by Christ at the Cross "that through death he might destroy him that had the power of death, that is, the devil" (Heb 2:14). Believers have already been "delivered from the power of darkness" and translated into the kingdom of God's dear Son (Col 1:13). Satan, then, should be treated as a defeated enemy. No longer has he any legitimate claim upon us. Once we were his lawful "captives" but now God works in us both to will and to do of His good pleasure. All that we now have to do is to "resist the devil," and the promise is, "he will flee from you" (Jam 4:7).

"It is finished." Here was the triumphant answer to the rage of man and the enmity of Satan. It tells of the perfect work which meets sin in the place of judgment. All was completed just as God would have it, just as the prophets had foretold, just as the Old Testament ceremonial had foreshadowed, just as divine holiness demanded, and just as sinners needed. How strikingly appropriate is this sixth Cross-utterance of the Savior found in John's Gospel, the Gospel which displays the glory of Christ's deity! He does not here commend His work to the approval of God, but seals it with His own imprimatur, attesting it is complete, and giving it the all-sufficient sanction of His own approval. None other than the Son of God says, "It is finished", who then dare doubt or question it.

"It is finished." Reader, do you believe it? or, are you trying to add something of your own to the finished work of Christ to secure the favour of God? All you have to do is to accept the pardon which He purchased. God is satisfied with the work of Christ, why are not you? Sinner, the moment you believe God's testimony concerning His beloved Son, that moment every sin you have committed is blotted out, and you stand accepted in Christ! O would you not like to possess the assurance that there is nothing between your soul and God? Would you not like to know that every sin had been atoned for and put away? Then believe what God's Word says about Christ's death. Rest not on your feelings and experiences but on the written Word. There is only one way of finding peace, and that is through faith in the shed blood of God's Lamb.

"It is finished." Do you really believe it? Or are you endeavouring to add something of your own to it and thus merit the favour of God? Some years ago, a Christian farmer was deeply concerned over an unsaved carpenter. The farmer sought to set before his neighbour the Gospel of God's grace, and to explain how that the finished work of Christ was sufficient for his soul to rest upon. But the carpenter persisted in the belief that he must do something himself. One day the farmer asked the carpenter to make for him a gate, and when the gate was ready, he carried it away to his wagon. He arranged for the carpenter to call on him the next morning and see the gate as it hung in the field. At the appointed hour the carpenter arrived and was surprised to find the farmer standing by with a sharp axe in his hand. "What are you going to do?" he asked. "I am going to add a few cuts and strokes to your work" was the response. "But there is no need for it," replied the carpenter, "the gate is alright as it is. I did all that was necessary to it." The farmer took no notice but lifting his axe he slashed and hacked at the gate until it was completely spoiled. "Look what you have done!" cried the carpenter, "you have ruined my work!" "Yes," said the farmer, "and that is what you are trying to do. You are seeking to nullify the finished work of Christ by your own miserable additions to it!" God used this forceful object lesson to show the carpenter his mistake, and he was led to cast himself by faith upon what Christ had done for sinners.

Reader, will you do the same?

7. The Word Of Contentment

"And when Jesus had cried with a loud voice, he said, Father, into your hands I commend my spirit: and having said thus, he gave up his spirit." Luke 23:46

"Father, into your hands I commend my spirit." These words set before us the last act of the Savior before He expired. It was an act of contentment, of faith, of confidence, and of love. The person to Whom He committed the precious treasure of His spirit was His own Father. Father is an encouraging and assuring title; well may a son commit any concern, however dear, into the hands of a father especially such a Son into the hands of such a Father.

That which was committed into the hands of the Father was His "spirit," which was on the point of being separated from the body. Scripture reveals man as a tripartite being: "spirit and soul and body" (1 Thessalonians 5:23). There is a difference between the soul and the spirit, though it is not easy to predicate wherein they are dissimilar. The spirit appears to be the highest part of our complex being. It is that which, particularly, distinguishes man from the beasts, and that which links him to God. The spirit is that which God forms within us (Zechariah 12:1) therefore is He called "The God of the spirits of all flesh" (Num 16:22). At death the spirit returns to God who gave it (Ecc 12:7). The act by which the Savior placed His spirit into the hands of the Father was an act of faith "I commend." It was a blessed act designed as a precedent for all His people. The last point observable is the manner in which Christ performed this act; He uttered those words "with a loud voice." He spoke that all might hear, and that His enemies who judged Him destitute and forsaken of God, might know it was not so any longer; but instead, that He was dear to His Father still, and could put His spirit confidently into His hands.

"Father, into Your hands I commend my spirit." This was the last utterance of the Savior before He expired. While He hung upon the Cross, seven times His lips moved in speech. Seven is the number of completeness of perfection. At Calvary then, as everywhere, the perfections of the Blessed One were displayed. Seven is also the number of rests in a finished work: in six days God made Heaven and earth and in the seventh He rested, contemplating with satisfaction that which He had pronounced "very good." So here with Christ: a work had been given Him to do, and that work was now done. Just as the sixth day brought the work of creation and reconstruction to a completion, so the sixth utterance of the Savior was "It is finished." And just as the seventh day was the day of rest and satisfaction, so the seventh utterance of the Savior brings Him to the place of rest, the Father's hands.

Seven times the dying Savior spoke. Three of His utterances concerned men: to one He gave the promise that he should be with Him that day in Paradise; to another He confided His mother; to the mass of spectators, He made mention of His thirst. Three of His utterances were addressed to God: to the Father He prayed for His murderers; to God He uttered His mournful plaint; and now into the hands of the Father He commends His spirit. In the hearing of God and men, angels, and devil, He had cried in triumph, "It is finished."

"Father, into your hands I commend my spirit." It is noteworthy that this closing cry of the Savior had been uttered by the Spirit of prophecy long centuries before the Incarnation. In the Thirty-first Psalm we hear David's Son and Lord saying, anticipatively, "In you, O

Lord, do I put my trust; let me never be ashamed: deliver me in your righteousness. Bow down your ear to me: deliver me speedily: be you my strong rock, for a house of defence to save me. For you are my rock and my fortress therefore, for your name's sake lead me and guide me. Pull me out of the net that they have laid privily for me: for you are my strength. Into your hand I commend my spirit: You have redeemed me, O Lord God of truth" (verses 1-5)!

In connection with each one of our Savior's cross-utterances, a prophecy was fulfilled. First, He cried, "Father, forgive them, for they know not what they do," and this fulfilled Isaiah 53:12: "made intercession for the transgressors." Secondly, He promised the thief, "Today shall you be with me in paradise," and this was a fulfilment of the prophecy of the angel to Joseph: "you shall call his name Jesus, for he shall save his people from their sins (Mat 1:21). Thirdly, to His mother He said, "Woman, behold your son," and this fulfilled the prophecy of Simeon: "A sword shall pierce through your own soul also" (Luke 2:35). Fourthly, He had asked, "My God, my God, why have you forsaken me?" and these were the identical words of Psalm 22:1. Fifthly, He exclaimed "I thirst," and this was in fulfilment of Psalm 69:21: "In my thirst they gave me vinegar to drink." Sixthly, He shouted in triumph, "It is finished," and these are almost the very words with which that wonderful Twenty-second Psalm concludes: "He had done," or, as the Hebrew might well be rendered, "He has finished," the context showing what He had done, namely, the work of atonement. Finally, He prayed, "Father, into your hands I commend my spirit," and, as we have shown above, He was but quoting as it had been written of Him beforehand in Psalm 31. O the wonders of the Cross! We shall never reach the end of them.

"Father, into your hands I commend my spirit."

1. Here we see the Savior back again in communion with the Father. This is exceedingly precious. For a while that communion was broken, broken outwardly, as the light of God's holy countenance was hidden from the Sin-bearer; but now the darkness had passed and was

ended forever. Up to the Cross there had been perfect and unbroken communion between the Father and the Son. It is exquisitely lovely to mark how the awful "cup" itself had been accepted from the Father's hand: "The cup which my Father has given me, shall I not drink it" (John 18:11). On the Cross, at the beginning, the Lord Jesus is still found in communion with the Father, for had He not cried, "Father, forgive them!" His first Cross-utterance, then, was "Father forgive," and now His last word is "Father into your hands I commend my spirit." But between those utterances He had hung there for six hours: three spent in sufferings at the hand of man and Satan; three spent in suffering at the hand of God, as the sword of divine justice was "awakened" to smite Jehovah's fellow. During those last three hours, God had withdrawn from the Savior, evoking that terrible cry, "My God, my God, why have you forsaken me?" But now it is all done. The cup is drained; the storm of wrath has spent itself; the darkness is past, and the Savior is seen once more in communion with the Father never more to be broken.

"Father." How often this word was upon the Savior's lips! His first recorded utterance was, "Knew you not that I must be about my Father's business?" In what was probably His first formal discourse, the Sermon on the Mount, He speaks of the "Father" seventeen times. While in His final discourse to the disciples, the "pascal discourse" found in John 14-16, the word "Father" is found no less than forty-five times! In the next chapter, John 17, which contains what is known as Christ's great high priestly prayer, He speaks to and of the Father six times more. And now the last time He speaks before He lays down His life, He says again, "Father, into your hands I commend my spirit."

And how blessed it is that His Father is our Father! Ours because His. How wonderful that is! How unspeakably precious that I can look up to the great and living God and say, "Father," my Father! What comfort is contained in this title! What assurance it conveys! God is my Father, then He loves me, loves me as He loves Christ Himself

(John 17:23)! God is my Father and loves me, then He cares for me. God is my Father and cares for me, then He will "supply all my need" (Phi 4:19). God is my Father, then He will see to it that no harm shall betide me, yes, that all things shall be made to work together for my good (Rom 8:28). O that His children entered more deeply and practically into the blessedness of this relationship, then would they joyfully exclaim with the apostle, "Behold, what manner of love the father has bestowed upon us, that we should be called the children of God" (1 John 3:1)!

"Father, into your hands I commend my spirit."

2. Here we see a designed contrast. For more than twelve hours Christ had been in the hands of men. Of this had He spoken to His disciples when He forewarned them that "The son of man shall be betrayed into the hands of men, and they shall kill him" (Mat 17:22-23). Of this had He made mention amid the awful solemnities of Gethsemane, "Then comes he to his disciples, and says unto them, Sleep on now, and take your rest: behold the hour is at hand, and the son of man is betrayed into the hands of sinners" (Mat 26:45). To this the angels had reference on the resurrection morning, saying to the women, "He is not here, but is risen: remember how he spoke unto you when he was yet in Galilee, saying, The son of man must be delivered into the hands of sinful men, and be crucified, and the third day rise again" (Luke 24:6-7).

This received its fulfilment when the Lord Jesus delivered Himself up to those who came to arrest Him in the Garden. As we saw in an earlier chapter, Christ could have easily avoided arrest. All He had to do was to leave the officers of the priests prostrate on the ground and walk quietly away. But He did not do so. The appointed hour had struck. The time when He should submit Himself to be led as a lamb to the slaughter had arrived. And He delivered Himself into "the hands of sinners." How they treated Him is well known; they took full advantage of their opportunity. They gave full vent to the hatred of the carnal heart for God. With "wicked hands" they crucified Him

(Act 2:23). But now all is over. Man has done his worst. The Cross has been endured; the appointed work is finished.

Voluntarily had the Savior delivered Himself into the hands of sinners, and now, voluntarily He delivers His spirit into the hands of the Father. What a blessed contrast! Never again will He be in "the hands of men." Never again will He be at the mercy of the wicked. Never again will He suffer shame. Into the hands of the Father, He commits Himself, and the Father will now look after His interests. We need not dwell at length on the blessed sequel. Three days later the Father raised Him from the dead. Forty days after that the Father exalted Him high above all principalities and powers and every name that is named and set Him at His own right hand in the Heavens. And there He now sits on the Father's throne (Rev 3:21), waiting until His enemies be made His footstool. For one day, before long, the tables shall be turned. The Father will send back the One Whom the world cast out send Him back in power and glory, send Him back to rule and reign over the whole earth with a rod of iron. There shall the situation be reversed. When He was here before, man dared to arraign Him, but then shall He sit and judge them. Once He was in their hands, then they shall be in His. Once they cried "away with him," then shall He say, "depart from me." And in the meantime, He is in the Father's hands, seated on His throne, awaiting His pleasure!

"Father, into your hands I commend my spirit: and having said thus, he gave up the spirit."

3. Here we see Christ's perfect yieldedness to God. How blessedly He evidenced this all the way through! When His mother sought Him in Jerusalem as a boy of twelve, He said, "Knew you not that I must be about my Father's business?" When a hungered in the wilderness after a forty-day fast, and the devil urged Him to make bread out of the stones, He lived by every word of God. When the mighty works which He had performed and the message He had delivered failed to move His auditors, He submitted to the One who had sent Him, saying, "I thank you, O Father, Lord of Heaven and earth, because

you have hid these things from the wise and prudent, and have revealed them unto babes" (Mat 11:25). When the sisters of Lazarus sent to the Savior to acquaint Him with the sickness of their brother, instead of hurriedly going to Bethany, He abode two days still in the place where He was, saying, "This sickness is not unto death but for the glory of God." It was not natural affections which moved Him to action, but the glory of God! His meat was to do the will of the One who sent Him.

In all things He submitted Himself to the Father. See Him in the morning, "rising up a great while before day" (Mar 1:35), in order that He might be in the presence of the Father. See Him anticipating every great crisis and preparing Himself for it by pouring out His heart in supplication. See Him spending the very last hour before His arrest on His face before God. How fitly might He say, "Take my yoke upon you, and learn of me; for I am meek and lowly in heart." And as He had lived, so He died, yielding Himself into the hands of the Father. This was the last act of the dying Savior. And how exquisitely beautiful! How thoroughly in keeping with the whole of His life! It manifested His perfect confidence in the Father. It revealed the blessed intimacy there was between Them. It exhibited His absolute dependency upon God.

Truly, in all things He has left us an example. The Savior committed His spirit into the hands of His Father in death, because it had been in the Father's hands all through His life! Is this true of you, my reader? Have you as a sinner committed your spirit into the hands of God? If so, it is in safe keeping. Can you say with the apostle, "I know whom I have believed, and am persuaded that he is able to keep that which I have committed unto him against that day" (2 Timothy 1:12)? And have you as a Christian fully yielded yourself to God? Have you heeded that word, "I beseech you therefore, brethren, by the mercies of God, that you present your bodies a living sacrifice, holy, acceptable to God, which is your reasonable service" (Rom 12:1)? Are you living for the glory of Him who loved you and gave Himself for you? Are you walking in daily dependence upon Him, knowing that without Him you can do nothing (John 15:5), but learning that you can do all things through Christ that strengthens you (Phi 4:13)! If your whole life is yielded up to God, and death should overtake you before the Savior returns to receive His people unto Himself, it will then be easy and natural for you to say, "Father, into your hands I commend my spirit." Balaam said, "Let me die the death of the righteous" (Num 23:10). Ah, but to die the death of the righteous, you must live the life of the righteous, and that consists in absolute submission to and dependency upon God.

"Father, into your hands I commend my spirit."

4. Here we see the absolute uniqueness of the Savior. The Lord Jesus died as none other ever did. His life was not taken from Him; He laid it down of Himself. This was His claim: "therefore does my Father love me, because I lay down my life, that I might take it again. No man takes it from me, but I lay it down myself. I have power to lay it down, and I have power to take it again" (John 10:17-18). The various proofs that Christ's life was not taken from Him have been set before the reader in the Introduction of this book. The most convincing evidence of all was seen in the committal of His spirit into the hands of the Father. The Lord Jesus Himself said, "Father, into your hands I commend my spirit." But the Holy Spirit, in describing the actual laying down of His life, has employed three different expressions which bring out very forcibly the fact we are now considering, and the various words used by the Spirit are most appropriate to the respective Gospels in which they are found.

In Matthew 27:50 we read, "And Jesus, when he had cried again with a loud voice, yielded up his spirit." But this translation fails to bring out the proper force of the original; the meaning of the Greek is, He "dismissed His spirit." The expression is most appropriate in Matthew, which is the kingly Gospel, presenting our Lord as "The son of David; the King of the Jews." Such a term is beautifully suited in the royal Gospel, for the Lord's act connotes one of authority, as of a king dismissing a servant.

The word used in Mark, which presents our Lord as the perfect Savior, is the same as in our text which is taken from Luke, the Gospel of Christ's perfect manhood. It signifies that He "breathed out His spirit." It was His passive endurance of death.

In John, which is the Gospel of Christ's divine glory, another word is employed by the Holy Spirit: "He bowed his head and gave up the spirit" (John 19:30), or "delivered up" would perhaps be more exact. Here the Savior does not "commend" His spirit to the Father, as in the Gospel of His humanity,11 but, in keeping with His divine glory, as One who has full power over it, He "delivers up" His spirit!

Two things were necessary in order to the making of atoning sacrifice: first, a complete satisfaction must be offered to God's outraged holiness and offended justice. And this, in the case of our Substitute, could only be by His suffering the outpoured wrath of God. And this [in fact] had been borne. Now there remained only the second thing, and that was for the Savior to taste of death. "It is appointed unto men once to die, but after this the judgment" (Heb 9:27). With the sinner it is death first, and then the judgment; with the Savior the order was, of course, reversed. He endured the judgment of God against our sins, and then He died.

The end was now reached. Perfect master of Himself, unconquered by death, He cries with a loud voice of unexhausted strength, and delivers up His spirit into the hands of His Father. In this, His uniqueness was manifested no one else ever did this or died thus. His birth was unique. His life was unique. His death also was unique. In "laying down" His life, His death was differentiated from all others' death. He died by an act of His own volition! Who but a divine Person could have done this? In a mere man it would have been suicide: but in Him it was a proof of His perfection and uniqueness. He died like the Prince of Life!

"Father, into your hands I commend my spirit."

5. Here we see the place of eternal security. Again, and again the Savior spoke of a people which had been "given" to Him (John 6:37, etc.), and at the hour of His arrest, He said, "Of them which you gave me have I lost none" (John 18:9). Then is it not lovely to see that in the hour of death, the blessed Savior commends them now into the safe keeping of the Father! On the Cross, Christ hung as the representative of His people, and therefore we view His last act as a representative one. When the Lord Jesus commended His spirit into the hands of His Father, He also presented our spirits along with His, to the Father's acceptance. Jesus Christ neither lived nor died for Himself, but for believers: what He did in this last act, referred to them as much as to Himself. We must look then on Christ as here gathering all the souls of the elect together, and making a solemn tender12 of them, with His own spirit to God.

The Father's hand is the place of eternal security. Into that hand the Savior committed His people, and there they are forever safe. Said Christ, referring to the elect, "My father which, gave them to me is greater than all: and none is able to pluck them out of my Father's hand" (John 10:29). Here then is the ground of the believer's confidence. Here is the basis of our assurance. Just as nothing could harm Noah when Jehovah's hand had secured the door of the ark, so nothing can touch the spirit of the saint which is grasped by the hand of Omnipotence. None can pluck us thence. Weak we are in ourselves, but "kept by the power of God" is the sure declaration of Holy Writ: "Kept by the power of God through faith unto salvation ready to be revealed in the last time" (1 Peter 1:5).

Formal professors, who seem to run well for a while, may grow weary and abandon the race. Those who are moved by the fleshly excitement of a "revival meeting," endure only for a time, for they have "no root in themselves." They who rely upon the power of their own wills and resolutions, who turn over a new leaf and promise to do better, often fail, and their last state is worse than the first. Many who have been persuaded by well meaning, but ignorant, advisers to "join the church" and "live the Christian life," frequently apostatize from the truth. But every spirit that has been born again is eternally safe in the Father's hand.

"Father, into your hands I commend my spirit."

6. Here we see the blessedness of communion with God. What we have reference to particularly is the fact that communion with God may be enjoyed independently of place or circumstances. The Savior was on the Cross, surrounded by a taunting crowd, His body suffering intense agony; nevertheless, He was in fellowship with the Father! This is one of the sweetest truths brought out by our text. It is our privilege to enjoy communion with God at all times, irrespective of outward circumstances or conditions. Communion with God is by faith, and faith is not affected by the things of sight. No matter how unpleasant your outward lot may be, my reader, it is your unspeakable privilege to enjoy communion with God. Just as the three Hebrews enjoyed fellowship with the Lord in the midst of the fiery furnace, as Daniel did in the lions' den, as Paul and Silas did in the Philippian jail, and as the Savior did on the Cross, so may you wherever you are! Christ's head rested on a crown of thorns, but beneath were the Father's hands!

Does not our text teach very pointedly the blessed truth and fact of communion with the Father in the hour of death! Then why dread it, fellow Christian? If David under the Old Testament dispensation could say, "Yes, though I walk through the valley of the shadow of death, I will fear no evil: for you are with me" (Psalm 23:4), why should believers now fear, after Christ has extracted the sting out of death! Death may be "king of terrors" to the unsaved, but to the Christian, death is simply the door which admits into the presence of the well Beloved. The motions of our souls in death, as in life, turn instinctively to God. "Father, into your hands I commend my spirit" will be our cry, if we are conscious. While we tabernacle here, we have no rest but in the bosom of God; and when we go hence, our expectation and earnest desires are to be with Him. We have cast many a longing look heavenwards; but when the soul of the saved nears the parting of the ways, then it throws itself into the arms of love, just as a river after many turnings and windings pours itself into the ocean. Nothing but God can satisfy our spirits in this world, and none but He can satisfy us as we go hence.

But reader, only believers are warranted and encouraged thus to commend their spirits into the hands of God at the dying hour; how sad is the state of all dying unbelievers. Their spirits, too, will fall into the hands of God, but this will be their misery, and not their privilege. These will find "It is a fearful thing to fall into the hands of the living God" (Heb 10:31). Yes, because instead of falling into the arms of Love, they will fall into the hands of Justice.

"Father, into your hands I commend my spirit."

7. Here we see the heart's true haven. If the closing utterance of the Savior expresses the prayer of dying Christians, it shows what great value they place on their spirits. The spirit within is the precious treasure, and our main solicitude and chief care is to see it secured in safe hands, "Father, into your hands I commend my spirit." These words then may be taken to express the believer's care for his soul: that it may be safe, whatever becomes of the body. God's saint who has come near to death, exercises few thoughts about his body, where it shall be laid, or how it shall be disposed of; he trusts that into the hands of his friends. But as his care all along has been his soul, so he thinks of it now, and with his last breath commits it to the custody of God. It is not, "Lord Jesus, receive my body," that is, "take care of my dust"; but rather, "Lord Jesus, receive my spirit" Lord, secure the jewel when the casket is broken.

And now a brief word of appeal in conclusion. My friend, you are in a world that is full of trouble. You are unable to take care of yourself in life, much less will you be able to do so in death. Life has many trials and temptations. Your soul is menaced from every side. On every hand are dangers and pitfalls. The world, the flesh, and the devil are combined against you; they are too much for your strength. Here then is the beacon of light amidst the darkness. Here is the harbour of shelter from all storms. Here is the blessed canopy which protects from all the fiery darts of the evil one. Thank God there is a refuge from the gales of life and from the terrors of death, the Father's hand, the heart's true haven.

"Father, into your hands I commend my spirit."

LIST OF TITLES WITH ISBN NO.

ISBN	TITLE
9788194914129	1984
9789390575220	1984 & Animal Farm (2In1)
9789390575572	1984 & Animal Farm (2In1): The International Best-Selling Classics
9789390575848	35 Sonnets
9789390575329	A Clergyman's Daughter
9789390575923	A Study In Scarlet
9789390896097	A Tale Of Two Cities
9789390896837	Abide in Christ
9789390896202	Abraham Lincoln
9789390896912	Absolute Surrender
9789390896608	African American Classic Collection
9789390575305	Aldous Huxley: The Collected Works
9789390896141	An Autobiography of M. K. Gandhi
9789390575886	Animal Farm
9789390575619	Animal Farm & The Great Gatsby (2In1)
9789390575626	Animal Farm & We
9789390896158	Anna Karenina
9789390575534	Antic Hay
9789390896165	Antony & Cleopatra
9789390896172	As I Lay Dying
9789390896226	As You like it
9789390575671	At Your Command
9789390575350	Awakened Imagination
9789390575114	Be What You Wish
9789390896233	Believe In yourself
9789390896998	Best of Charles Darwin: The Origin of Species & Autobiography
9789390896684	Best Of Horror : Dracula And Frankenstein
9789390575503	Best Of Mark Twain (The Adventures of Tom Sawyer AND The Adventures of Huckleberry Finn)
9789390896769	Black History Collection
9789390575756	Brave New World, Animal Farm & 1984 (3in1)

9789390896240	Brother Karamzov
9789390575053	Bulleh Shah Poetry
9789390575725	Burmese Days
9789390896257	Bushido
9789390896066	Can't Hurt Me
9788194914112	Chanakya Neeti: With The Complete Sutras
9789390896042	Crime and Punishment
9789390575527	Crome Yellow
9789390575046	Down and Out in Paris and London
9789390896844	Dracula
9789390575442	Emersons Essays: The Complete First & Second Series (Self-Reliance & Other Essays)
9789390575749	Emma
9789390575817	Essential Tozer Collection - The Pursuit of God & The Purpose of Man
9789390896578	Fascism What It Is and How to Fight It
9789390575688	Feeling is the Secret
9789390575190	Five Lessons
9789390575954	Frankenstein
9789390575237	Franz Kafka: Collected Works
9789390575282	Franz Kafka: Short Stories
9789390575060	George Orwell Collected Works
9789390575077	George Orwell Essays
9789390575213	George Orwell Poems
9788194914150	Greatest Poetry Ever Written Vol 1
9788194914143	Greatest Poetry Ever Written Vol 1
9789390896301	Gulliver's Travel
9789390575961	Gunaho Ka Devta
9789390575893	H. P. Lovecraft Selected Stories Vol 1
9789390575978	H. P. Lovecraft Selected Stories Vol 2
9789390896059	Hamlet
9789390575022	His Last Bow: Some Reminiscences of Sherlock Holmes
9789390896134	History of Western Philosophy
9789390575121	Homage To Catalonia

9789390896219	How to develop self-confidence and Improve public Speaking
9789390896295	How to enjoy your life and your Job
9789390575633	How to own your own mind
9789390896318	How to read Human Nature
9789390896325	How to sell your way through the life
9789390896370	How to use the laws of mind
9789390896387	How to use the power of prayer
9789390896028	How to win friends & Influence People
9788194824176	How To Win Friends and Influence People
9789390896103	Humility The Beauty of Holiness
9789390896653	Imperialism the Highest Stage of Capitalism
9789390575084	In Our Time
9789390575169	In Our Time & Three Stories and Ten poems
9789390575145	James Allen: The Collected Works
9789390896189	Jesus Himself
9789390575480	Jo's Boys
9789390896394	Julius Caesar
9789390575404	Keep the Aspidistra Flying
9789390896400	Kidnapped
9789390896424	King Lear
9789390575824	Lady Susan
9789390896455	Law of Success
9789390896264	Lincoln The Unknown
9789390575565	Little Men
9789390575640	Little Women
9788194914174	Lost Horizon
9789390896462	Macbeth
9789390896929	Man Eaters of Kumaon
9789390896523	Man The Dwelling Place of God
9789390896349	Man The Dwelling Place of God
9789390575909	Mansfield Park
9788194914136	Manto Ki 25 Sarvshreshth Kahaniya
9789390896509	Marxism, Anarchism, Communism
9789390575664	Mathematical Principles of Natural Philosophy

9788194914198	Meditations
9789390575800	Mein Kampf
9789390575794	Memory How To Develop, Train, And Use It
9789390896486	Mind Power
9789390896585	Money
9789390575039	Mortal Coils
9789390575770	My Life and Work
9789390896035	Narrative of the Life of Frederick Douglass
9789390575152	Neville Goddard: The Collected Works
9789390575985	Northanger Abbey
9789390896530	Notes From Underground
9789390896547	Oliver Twist
9789390575459	On War
9789390575541	One, None and a Hundred Thousand
9789390896554	Othelo
9789390575435	Out Of This World
9789390575015	Persuasion
9789390575510	Prayer The Art Of Believing
9789390575091	Pride and Prejudice
9789390896561	Psychic Perception
9789390575381	Rabindranath Tagore - 5 Best Short Stories Vol 2
9789390575367	Rabindranath Tagore - Short Stories (Masters Collections Including The Childs Return)
9789390575374	Rabindranath Tagore 5 Best Short Stories Vol 1 (Including The Childs Return
9789390896622	Romeo & Juliet
9789390896127	Sanatana Dharma
9789390575596	Seedtime & Harvest
9789390896639	Selected Stories of Guy De Maupassant
9789390575206	Self-Reliance & Other Essays
9789390575176	Sense and Sensibility
9789390575299	Shyamchi Aai
9789390896738	Socialism Utopian and Scientific
9789390896646	Success Through a Positive Mental Attitude
9789390575428	The Adventures of Huckleberry Finn

9789390575183	The Adventures of Sherlock Holmes
9789390575343	The Adventures of Tom Sawyer
9789390896691	The Alchemy Of Happiness
9789390575862	The Art Of Public Speaking
9789390896288	The Autobiography Of Charles Darwin
9788194914181	The Best of Franz Kafka: The Metamorphosis & The Trial
9789390575008	The Call Of Cthulhu and Other Weird Tales
9789390575107	The Case-Book of Sherlock Holmes
9789390896110	The Castle Of Otranto
9789390896745	The Communist Manifesto
9789390575589	The Complete Fiction of H. P. Lovecraft
9789390575497	The Complete Works of Florence Scovel Shinn
9789390896820	The Conquest of Breard
9789390896813	The Diary of a Young Girl
9789390896332	The Diary of a Young Girl The Definitive Edition of the Worlds Most Famous Diary
9789390575701	The Great Gatsby, Animal Farm & 1984 (3In1)
9789390575312	The Greatest Works Of George Orwell (5 Books) Including 1984 & Non-Fiction
9789390575992	The Hound of Baskervilles
9789390896707	The Idiot
9789390896714	The Invisible Man
9789390575657	The Knowledge of the holy
9789390575558	The Law & the Promise
9789390896721	The Law Of Attraction
9789390896776	The Leader in you
9789390896363	The Life of Christ
9789390896196	The Man-Eating Leopard of Rudraprayag
9789390896783	The Master Key to Riches
9789390575268	The Memoirs Of Sherlock Holmes
9789390896479	The Midsummer Night's Dream
9789390575466	The Mill On The Floss
9789390896790	The Miracles of your mind
9789390896660	The Mutual Aid A Factor in Evolution
9789390896448	The Origin of Species

9789390896905	The Peter Kropotkin Anthology The Conquest of Bread & Mutual Aid A Factor of Evolution
9789390896806	The Picture of Dorian Gray
9789390896271	The Picture of Dorian Gray
9789390575275	The Power Of Awareness
9789390896356	The Power of Concentration
9788194824169	The Power of Positive Thinking
9789390575411	The Power of the Spoken Word
9788194914105	The Power Of Your Subconscious Mind
9789390896899	The Power of Your Subconscious Mind
9789390896417	The Principles of Communism
9789390575787	The Psychology Of Mans Possible Evolution
9789390896615	The Psychology of Salesmanship
9789390575732	The Pursuit of God
9789390575398	The Pursuit of Happiness
9789390896851	The Quick and Easy Way to effective Speaking
9789390575947	The Return Of Sherlock Holmes
9789390575138	The Road To Wigan Pier
9789390896981	The Root of the Righteous
9789390575855	The Science Of Being Well
9788194914167	The Science Of Getting Rich, The Science Of Being Great & The Science Of Being Well (3In1)
9789390896011	The Screwtape Letters
9789390896073	The Screwtape Letters
9789390575336	The Secret Door to Success
9789390575695	The Secret Of Imagining
9789390896868	The Secret Of Success
9789390896431	The Seven Last Words
9789390575930	The Sign of the Four
9789390896004	The Sonnets
9789390896516	The Souls of Black Folk
9789390896875	The Sound and The Fury
9789390575244	The State and Revolution
9789390896882	The Story of My Life
9789390896936	The Story Of Oriental Philosophy

9789390896752	The Strange Case of Dr. Jekyll and Mr. Hyde
9789390896943	The Tempest
9789390575916	The Valley Of Fear
9789390575879	The Wind in the willows
9789390896080	The Wind in the willows
9789390575763	Their eyes were watching gofd
9789390575831	Three Stories
9789390896950	Twelfth Night
9789390896592	Twelve Years a Slave
9789390896677	Up from Slavery
9789390896974	Value Price and Profit
9789390896967	Wake Up and Live
9789390896493	With Christ in the School of Prayer
9789390575602	Your Faith is Your Fortune
9789390575473	Your Infinite Power To Be Rich
9789390575251	Your Word is Your Wand
9789390575718	Youth
9789391316099	A Christmas Carol
9789391316105	A Doll's House
9789391316501	A Passage to India
9789391316709	A Portrait of the Artist as a Young Man
9789391316112	A Tale of Two Cities
9789391316747	A Tear and a Smile
9789391316167	Agnes Gray
9789391316174	Alice's Adventures in Wonderland
9789391316136	Anandamath
9789391316181	Anne Of Green Gables
9789391316754	Anthem
9789391316198	Around The World in 80 Days
9789391316013	As A Man Thinketh
9789391316242	Autobiography of a Yogi
9789391316266	Beyond Good and Evil
9789391316761	Bleak House
9789391316778	Chitra, a Play in One Act
9789391316310	David Copperfield

9789391316075	Demian
9789391316785	Dubliners
9789391316051	Favourite Tales from the Arabian Nights
9789391316235	Gitanjali
9789391316068	Gravity
9789391316150	Great Speeches of Abraham Lincoln
9789391316662	Guerilla Warfare
9789391316839	Kim
9789391316822	Mother
9789391316211	My Childhood
9789391316846	Nationalism
9789391316327	Oliver Twist
9789391316853	Pygmalion
9789391316334	Relativity: The Special and the General Theory
9789391316389	Scientific Healing Affirmation
9789391316341	Sons and Lovers
9789391316587	Tales from India
9789391316372	Tess of The D'Urbervilles
9789391316396	The Awakening and Selected Stories
9789391316402	The Bhagvad Gita
9789391316303	The Book of Enoch
9789391316228	The Canterville Ghost
9789391316907	The Dynamic Laws of Prosperity
9789391316006	The Great Gatsby
9789391316860	The Hungry Stones and Other Stories
9789391316433	The Idiot
9789391316440	The Importance of Being Earnest
9789391316297	The Light of Asia
9789391316914	The Madman His Parables and Poems
9789391316457	The Odyssey
9789391316921	The Picture of Dorian Gray
9789391316464	The Prince
9789391316938	The Prophet
9789391316945	The Republic
9789391316518	The Scarlet Letter

9789391316143	The Seven Laws of Teaching
9789391316525	The Story of My Experiments with Truth
9789391316532	The Tales of the Mother Goose
9789391316549	The Thirty Nine Steps
9789391316594	The Time Machine
9789391316600	The Turn of the Screw
9789391316983	The Upanishads
9789391316617	The Yellow Wallpaper
9789391316426	The Yoga Sutras of Patanjali
9789391316990	Ulysses
9789391316624	Utopia
9789391316679	Vanity Fair
9789391316020	What Is To Be Done
9789391316686	Within A Budding Grove
9789391316693	Women in Love

www.ingramcontent.com/pod-product-compliance
Lightning Source LLC
LaVergne TN
LVHW101923220826
846093LV00009B/346

* 9 7 8 9 3 9 4 9 2 4 0 8 6 *